The
INVISIBLE THREAD

Going Where No Man Has Gone Before

PASTOR LORRAINE DAVIS

ISBN 979-8-88685-677-4 (paperback)
ISBN 979-8-88685-678-1 (digital)

Christian Faith Publishing
832 Park Avenue
Meadville, PA 16335
www.christianfaithpublishing.com

Printed in the United States of America

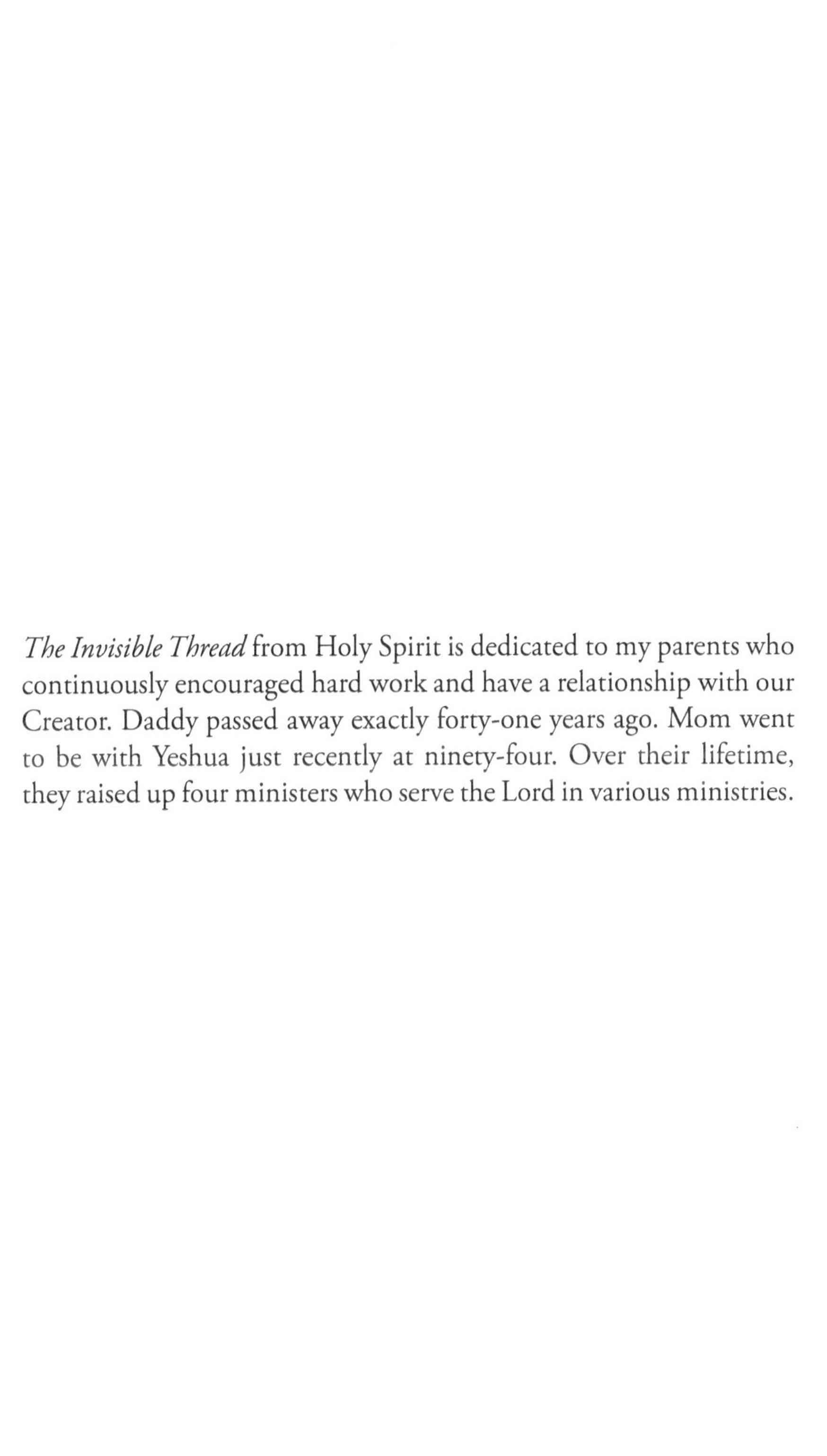

The Invisible Thread from Holy Spirit is dedicated to my parents who continuously encouraged hard work and have a relationship with our Creator. Daddy passed away exactly forty-one years ago. Mom went to be with Yeshua just recently at ninety-four. Over their lifetime, they raised up four ministers who serve the Lord in various ministries.

This book recognizes the love-filled blood covenant given in the beginning and how we can access the tools of the covenant relationship. A very easy read while learning more about ourselves in the process. *"Call unto me, and I will answer thee, and show thee great and mighty things which thou know not"* (Jeremiah 33:3 KJV).

MANUSCRIPT NOTATION

In the manuscript, the name of our heavenly Father has been changed from the Lord to His Hebrew personal name, Yahovah. The name of God, which is a title, has been changed when referring to the attribute of Creator, Elohim. The name of the Son of God, Jesus Christ, has been also stated as His Hebrew name, Yeshua or Yeshua Ha Messiah. The name Jesus or Yeshua and God or Lord are used interchangeably. This includes scriptures where quoting Satan's name is never capitalized unless at the beginning of a sentence.

> In Elohim is my salvation and my glory; The rock
> of my strength, And my refuge, is in Elohim.
> (Psalm 62:7 NKJV)

CONTENTS

Preface..xi

Introduction..xiii

Who Are We 1

In the Beginning 10

Covenant...13

Books of Remembrance..25

Courts of Heaven...28

The Word of God 31

The Name of God 38

The Names of Yeshua 45

Covenant Rights and Benefits 47

Communion 49

Tithing...53

Pentecost 58

The Power of the Shofar..62

We Are Loved...68

Discover Judaism's Truth 71

Praise and Worship...74

Covenant Authority..78

The Prayer of Agreement 84

Healing 87

Keys of the Kingdom...92

Gifts of the Spirit 96

Fruit of the Spirit 103

Redemption 106

Prophetic Dreams..108

The Weak Christian Condition 114

Life and Death 123
Spiritual Brokenness...125
Angels 129
Sin 134
The "Job" Challenge..143
Faith..145
Spiritual Relationships...154
Is Seeing Believing? 158
Life's Brokenness 162
Another Night with the Frogs...165

Preface

After spending eighteen days in the hospital, ten on the respirator, my whole perspective on heaven, relationship, and Yahovah's kingdom changed. I saw things from His view and not always from the earth's natural circumstances. Dying can change a great deal of your thinking!

I had written a couple of books; wanting to write another book I needed a title. My younger brother Bob suggested "The Invisible Thread." It immediately drew me into the underlying concept of the scarlet cord of Rahab in Joshua 2:18. I began to write what was on my heart. The Holy Spirt began to give me unction. The covenant has always appealed to my love of biblical history, as well as understanding how to apply the principles in daily living. The invisible thread of love, blood covenant, and redemption all come together in searchable mysteries of the Holy Word of God.

> I will stand my watch and set myself on the rampart, And watch to see what He will say to me, And what I will answer when I am corrected. The Just Live by Faith. Then Yahovah answered me and said: "Write the vision and make it plain on tablets, that he may run who reads it." (Habakkuk 2:1–2 NKJV)

INTRODUCTION

Before the dawn of creation, there has always been an invisible thread that connects us with our Creator. His plan existed before He threw out the stars, called into existence a planet for humanity to live on or a promise lasting as long as seed time and harvest. Yahovah started a process whereby we can absolutely depend on Him for every possible need, desire or provision called a love-filled blood covenant. His covenant has given us tools, gifts, benefits, and provisions. When we fully understand what has been secured for us, we cannot just survive but thrive in the attributes of His everlasting love. God's extravagant unending love invites us, His creation, to participate in a dance in His love affair with us.

> Open my eyes, that I may see wondrous things
> from Your law. (Psalm 119:18 NKJV)

Who Are We

Yahovah's love created us with a plan in place, building, trusting He can and will always have our best at His heart and the best for ours. The only way we can learn to trust His love is reading His Word, spending quality time with Him, living faithfully by listening to Holy Spirit. He continually gives us guidance and instruction. If we are accepted in the beloved as in Ephesians 1:6, then it is our duty, obligation, and love journey to find what our path is. Psalm 139:16 NKJV says in essence, He already knows us. It's in His book. "Your eyes saw my substance, being yet unformed. And in Your book they all were written, the days fashioned for me, when as yet there were none of them."

The Passion Translation (TPT) says it even more plainly. "You saw who you created me to be before I became me! Before I'd ever seen the light of day, the number of days you planned for me was already recorded in your book" (Psalm 139:16). I heard one teacher say in the womb, God's own fingers are shaping our being to be what His love desires for us. He writes it in a book for each of us. We are not an accident but a part of His eternal plan for our lives. I heard Yeshua once tell me He has sent many prophets, teachers, preachers, scientists, and world leaders to have them aborted before their assignments could be filled. The adversary devised the evil destroying our youth. World policies, unethical education programs, and weak religious teaching have given the enemy an open door to intentionally damage the kingdom of God. God has a plan, but He gave dominion to man who has taken our authority, using it to fulfill the challenger of the faith's evil strategy. Man is the key. He either submits to God or succumbs to the designs of the enemy.

During the extended time spent in the hospital, the verse in Psalm 139:16 kept going over and over in my mind. One learns just how vulnerable and tenuous or fragile life can be, recognizing the value of every breath, every moment His grace stretches, giving another day to live. He gave me back life. I was given five medications; each separately could have caused death. I died. But God had other plans. This is no wasted life. We have such amazing grace in a relationship fulfilling, intimate, and definitely full of life, love, and abundant blessing. We are in covenant relationship with our King/Creator. As I lay absolutely helpless, not able to move even a finger or to speak above a whisper, I did not know where I was, how I got there or why.

Yahovah began to speak to me in an audible voice. He said He had birthed me for an assignment. I ask, "You mean like Sarah and Mary?"

His laughing response was "Well, not exactly." He explained to me this assignment was one only I could do. When it came time, I would know what it was and what to do. I drifted back to sleep once again into the paralytic coma quiet I had been in for ten days.

While still in the hospital, days later, I remember being in His presence, feeling the wind in my hair as I traveled the universe with the Creator. I saw things in space I had never seen in books, movies, or my well-used imagination. We had several conversations where I asked hard questions; He indulged me with answers. I started to leave this experience out; but recently, at 2:00 a.m., I was once again in His presence. I asked about the book. He told me I had left things out that needed to be added. "Remind my children, I made the universe to share spiritually with *my* family." Like Spock on the USS Enterprise as he looks out the forward observation window and asked Captain Kirk, "Where do we go?" His response was the same as Elohim's. "Out there, where no man has gone before. Engage." His finger pointed outward toward the window. We limit ourselves to the few feet of ground under our feet, thinking it's all there is. Not so. He told me He wants to share His universe. "Be creative in your imagination." Our creative God gave us His Creativity.

Yahovah told Abram to look up and count the stars; Abram looked up at those same stars, planets, and immense space. The scene hasn't changed, but our perspective of the vastness of it all has. We can sit on the Master's shoulder, feel the wind in our hair, travel the universe of creative ideas, begin to experience the bigness of our God. I believe He would have us enjoy our relationship not just don't, don't, don't.

My first nights actually awake from the coma, I had the same dream two consecutive nights. I dreamed a small leafy plant I helped plant grew. When I turned around, it became a whole field full of plants as far as the eye could see. As I walked away from the garden, I was suddenly attacked by a being with a thousand eyes. Somehow I gathered up the corners of the sky and flung the whole thing into outer space and declared, "I belonged to Yeshua Ha Messiah, and you [the being] had no right or authority in my life." The first night I believe there was an actual battle in the spirit, but I didn't have the strength to understand. The second night, I acknowledged my authority and acted.

I had several more encounters with Yahovah in the nights following. Some of which were as real as my car in the driveway. I know without a shadow of a doubt, He was teaching me of His extravagant, magnificent love, relationship, and authority. I saw the universe from a whole different perspective. It was vast with planets, stars, and cosmic movements; it was His playground. I heard Him say, "We have our playgrounds in our dimension, and He has his." It has changed my life dramatically. I preached Lazarus and I have a lot in common: we both rose from the dead, we went about telling everyone, and we were never the same again.

Too many in today's world spend time in church but little time in the presence of the Creator. Our time in His Word is more valuable than the air we breathe. Church buildings are not what make an ecclesia or the governing body on the earth. The family of God is a living entity; when in agreement, will move mountains, bring justice in the courts of heaven, and deliver healing where only the Great Physician can operate.

I once had a dream of being cowered down behind a large rock in a major battle. I was waiting for my next order. Suddenly, a captain I did not recognize in the early dawn came up beside me. I stated I did not recognize Him, to which he responded, "You know me, I am Captain Victory. Just press in a little harder." Listening to our Captain gives us assurance, He is listening to our every prayer, waiting and willing to answer our requests.

Yeshua can be found throughout the Scriptures by recognizing He existed before time. History places Him in a two-thousand-year-old story as a baby, a young man of twelve, and finally a short ministry. His twelve disciples didn't fully understand who was walking, talking, and leading them.

The pattern of the tabernacle with the sacrifices, atonement, and blood shout out the pattern of redemption. Sacrifices had to be repeated daily and yearly. The blood of Yeshua provided a one time everlasting experience of redemption, grace, and hope. Even some church members have a hard time believing the Son of everlasting God came to earth to be as we are, to live as we do, undergoing the same temptations, experiencing humanity. His humanity gave Yeshua knowledge to understand our whole lifetime of temptations, emotions, grief, and disappointments. He took His own blood into the Holy of Holies. The unsurpassed value paid it all—it is *finished!*

To understand the implications of the term *it is finished* one must look at both the Hebrew/Aramaic and Greek words. Since the return from Babylon nearly one thousand years earlier, most Jews spoke Aramaic. The Hebrew word pronounced *kalah* (Strong's word 3615) defines the action Yeshua shouted at His death. It is finished, accomplished as planned, debt legally paid in full. As Yahovah finished (*kalah* 3615) creation in Genesis 2:1–2, Yeshua finished or completed the redemptive plan.

The whole chapter of Psalm 22 was prophetically written of His death by King David. Over Yeshua's head was written a sign in Aramaic which stated Yeshua Hanozri Wumelech a Yehudim, which is YHVH—Yeshua, the Nazarene, King of the Jews. Another words, Yahovah's Son in the flesh was on the cross giving His life for ours. (W is pronounced as V in Aramaic and Hebrew.)

Yeshua completed, *kalal*, accomplished all he was sent to do. The Greek word *tetelestia* (Strong's word 5055) finished the task, goal, or purpose of the plan created pre-man. *It is finished!*

> Therefore My Father loves Me, because I lay down My life that I may take it again. No one takes it from Me, but I lay it down of Myself. I have power to lay it down, and I have power to take it again. This command I have received from My Father. (John 10:17–18 NKJV)

> For this reason the Father loves Me, because I lay down My [own] life so that I may take it back. No one takes it away from Me, but I lay it down voluntarily. I am authorized and have power to lay it down and to give it up, and I am authorized and have power to take it back. This command I have received from My Father. (John 10:17–18 AMP)

Isaiah 52:13–15 (KJV) declares there would come one who would die, and they would finally see the plan established and revealed from the beginning in Genesis 3:15, "*And I will put enmity between thee and the woman, and between thy seed and her seed; it shall bruise thy head, and thou shalt bruise his heel.*"

> Behold, my servant shall deal prudently, he shall be exalted and extolled, and be very high. As many were astounded at thee; his visage was so marred more than any man, and his form more than the sons of men: So shall he sprinkle many nations; the kings shall shut their mouths at him: for that which had not been told them shall they see; and that which they had not heard shall they consider. (Isaiah 52:13–15)

Isaiah 53:1–12 prophesies Yeshua, His life, death, and fulfillment of the Old Covenant prophecies.

> Who hath believed our report? And to whom is the arm of Yahovah revealed? For he shall grow up before him as a tender plant, and as a root out of a dry ground: he hath no form or comeliness; and when we shall see him, there is no beauty that we should desire him. He is despised and rejected of men; a man of sorrows, and acquainted with grief: and we hid as it were our faces from him; he was despised, and we esteemed him not. Surely he hath borne our griefs, and carried our sorrows: yet we did esteem him stricken, smitten of Elohim, and afflicted. But he was wounded for our transgressions; he was bruised for our iniquities: the chastisement of our peace was upon him; and with his stripes we are healed. All we like sheep have gone astray; we have turned everyone to his own way; and Yahovah hath laid on him the iniquity of us all. He was oppressed, and he was afflicted, yet he opened not his mouth: he is brought as a lamb to the slaughter, and as a sheep before her shearers is dumb, so he opens not his mouth. He was taken from prison and from judgment: and who shall declare his generation? For he was cut off out of the land of the living: for the transgression of my people was he stricken. And he made his grave with the wicked and with the rich in his death; because he had done no violence, neither was any deceit in his mouth. Yet it pleased Yahovah to bruise him; he hath put him to grief: when thou shalt make his soul an offering for sin, he shall see his seed, he shall prolong his days, and the pleasure of Yahovah shall prosper in his hand. He shall see of the travail of his

soul, and shall be satisfied: by his knowledge shall my righteous servant justify many; for he shall bear their iniquities. Therefore will I divide him a portion with the great, and he shall divide the spoil with the strong; because he hath poured out his soul unto death: and he was numbered with the transgressors; and he bare the sin of many, and made intercession for the transgressors.

Yeshua became sin in our place. He paid the price for our redemption, destroying the self-imposed authority of the adversary.

> The one who practices sin [separating himself from God, and offending Him by acts of disobedience, indifference, or rebellion] is of the devil [and takes his inner character and moral values from him, not God]; for the devil has sinned and violated God's law from the beginning. The Son of God appeared for this purpose, to destroy the works of the devil. (1 John 3:8 AMP)

Yeshua stated in John 5:30 (AMP) He was fulfilling the will of the Father. "*I can do nothing on my own initiative or authority. Just as I hear, I judge; and My judgment is just [fair, righteous, unbiased], because I do not seek My own will, but only the will of Him who sent Me.*"

> So they said to Him, "Who are You [anyway]?" Jesus replied, "What have I been saying to you from the beginning? I have many things to say and judge concerning you, but He who sent Me is true; and I say to the world [only] the things that I have heard from Him." They did not realize [or have the spiritual insight to understand] that He was speaking to them about the Father. So Jesus said, "When you lift up the Son of Man [on the

cross], you will know then [without any doubt] that I am He, and that I do nothing on My own authority, but I say these things just as My Father taught Me. And He who sent Me is [always] with Me; He has not left Me alone, because I always do what pleases Him." (John 8:25–29 AMP)

But in those sacrifices there is a remembrance again made of sins every year. For it is not possible that the blood of bulls and of goats should take away sins. Wherefore when he cometh into the world, he says, Sacrifice and offering thou would not, but a body hast thou prepared me: in burnt offerings and sacrifices for sin thou hast had no pleasure. Then said I, Lo, I come (in the volume of the book it is written of me,) to do thy will, O Elohim. Above when he said, Sacrifice and offering and burnt offerings and offering for sin thou would not, neither had pleasure therein; which are offered by the law; Then said he, Lo, I come to do thy will, O Elohim. He taketh away the first that he may establish the second. By which will we are sanctified through the offering of the body of Jesus Christ once for all. (Hebrews 10:3–10 KJV)

What happened on that fateful day? The war in the heavens affected the earth with both kingdoms struggling as Yeshua becomes Master of the universe. The sky turned black for three hours: The earth shook. Graves opened. The veil in the temple was rent, and many captives were released. Yeshua secured the keys to the kingdom by outwitting the adversary at his own game by appearing in Sheol, next to the devil's lair. When the battle was over, Yeshua had the keys of the kingdom, defeated death, hell, the grave, and rose rightfully to everlasting victory over darkness and sin. He *finished* the war!

Jesus, when He had cried again with a loud voice, yielded up the ghost. And, behold, the veil of the temple was rent in twain from the top to the bottom; and the earth did quake, and the rocks rent; And the graves were opened; and many bodies of the saints which slept arose, And came out of the graves after His resurrection, and went into the holy city, and appeared unto many. Now when the centurion, and they that were with him, watching Yeshua, saw the earthquake, and those things that were done, they feared greatly, saying, truly this was the Son of Yahovah. (Matthew 27:50–56 KJV)

In the Beginning

When Adam walked with Elohim in the Garden of Eden, he personally knew the extravagant love extended to all creation. It would have been a horrible shock to realize the consequences of his agreement with the accuser and treasonous betrayal of that love. Two lambs he had just name a few hours ago were suddenly slaughtered. They watched as the love-filled Father skinned the animals and placed their bloody skins upon their backs, then sent Adam and his wife out of the garden forever, The first blood covenant originated by love.

The essence of the blood covenant through all eternity proves love as a method to *not* continue in sin. Leviticus 7:11 (KJV) states the life is in the blood. *"For the life of the flesh is in the blood: and I have given it to you upon the altar to make atonement for your souls: for it is the blood that makes atonement for the soul."*

This is repeated in Hebrews 9:22 (KJV), *"And almost all things are by the law purged with blood; and without shedding of blood is no remission."*

Adam and Eve would have taught their sons the value of the sacrifice atoning for their transgression. It was not an accident that Cain's sacrifice was not accepted. He was choosing his own method of approaching Elohim rather than the pattern set by the Creator Himself. Religion is as old as the first humans trying to change God's original plan, trying to be approved, trying to return to the love relationship with rules, to-do lists, and falling short in every fashion.

> And in vain they worship Me, Teaching as doctrines the commandments of men for laying aside the commandment of Elohim, you hold the tradition of men—the washing of pitchers and cups,

and many other such things you do. He said to them, "All too well you reject the commandment of Elohim, that you may keep your tradition. For Moses said, 'Honor your father and your mother'; and, 'He who curses father or mother, let him be put to death.' But you say, 'If a man says to his father or mother, "Whatever profit you might have received from me is Corban" (that is, a gift to God), "then you no longer let him do anything for his father or his mother, making the Word of Elohim of no effect through your tradition which you have handed down. And many such things you do." (Mark 7:7–13 NKJV)

I recently had a dream of sitting on the side in a small church with old wooden pews. Slowly a dark presence appeared in the church through the open door, hovering over the congregation. Before even comprehending what was happening, I saw a small girl suddenly rise up, then a woman, and finally a man taken from life. I screamed, "Stop," when the dark presence turned as if to look my way but reached for another victim. I shouted, "By the blood of Yeshua, be gone." It immediately disappeared from the room. The Lord reminded me the only element producing immediate results was the blood that was shed on Calvary for our benefit, GRACE (God's riches at Christ's expense). I was reminded to always speak of the blood.

I once heard a woman say she didn't believe in "pleading the blood." Obviously, misunderstanding of the legal transaction performed in heaven gave doubt about the power of the blood. Yeshua didn't just die. He paid a legal price for our sins. Adam traded his dominion and rights to the accuser as it was misrepresented to Eve in the garden. Hebrews 8:6 tells us that Yeshua is the mediator of a better covenant.

But now Yeshua the Messiah has accepted a priestly ministry which far surpasses theirs, since He the catalyst of a better covenant which contains a far more wonderful promises. (Hebrews 8:6 TPT)

A mediator is as a district attorney (DA) stating the case before the judge while the prosecuting attorney (PA), the accuser, gives all the reasons for guilt. The PA supports the facts, a legal case against each of us. He knows all the facts in full detail; but the blood of Yeshua speaks giving us a victorious verdict. The judge hears Yeshua's blood speak just as Abel's blood spoke before Yahovah outside of the garden. The blood of Yeshua now speaks for us when we accept redemption, bought with His blood, and enrolled into the family of God. Now when we stand before the judge, Yahovah does not hear the sin; He hears the blood through Yeshua speak for us. The covenant stands.

> Yahovah said, "What have you done? The voice of your brother's [innocent] blood is crying out to Me from the ground [for justice]". (Genesis 4:10 AMP)

> By faith Abel offered unto Elohim a more excellent sacrifice than Cain, by which he obtained witness that he was righteous, Elohim testifying of His gifts: and by it he being dead yet speaks. But without faith it is impossible to please Him: for he that cometh to God must believe that He is, and that He is a rewarder of them that diligently seek Him. (Hebrews 11:4, 6 KJV)

Just as we use specific tools to work the field—rake, hoe, shovel, planters, harvesters—we have tools for the garden of our faith. We have tools, gifts, and benefits to apply provisions to every need, including healing, restoration, deliverance, and peace that passes understanding. The tools of our faith are spiritual, not physical, prayer of agreement, binding and loosing, and many more. The believer has many tools he can rely on to build and reinforce faith as we venture forth into the many facets of the Word of the living God.

COVENANT

You may be asking just what a covenant is. A covenant is *not* a contract. A contact by definition has a beginning and an ending—car, house, major purchase—paid in full, purchase completed. A contract is totally opposite of a covenant. Contracts demonstrate a lack of trust, lack of agreement, even a lack of equal partners. If a contract is violated, it becomes void. It must be reestablished to continue.

A covenant is defined as a legally binding life-and-death agreement between two partners ending only with death. It is a seal between two or more parties. In a biblical sense, the Hebrew word pronounced *Bret* or covenant derives from the same root word meaning "to cut," Strong's no. 1285. This means that in the culture of the Bible, a covenant carried full weight and was cut, or sealed, in blood, an oath. Covenants denote one giving oneself totally to the other. All I have is yours, and all you have is mine. The only way a covenant is broken is to not obey the conditions. To renew it, you only need to be obedient to it again. If I falter, I give myself unto death. Yahovah, on the other hand, cannot falter in any fashion, or He would cease to be the Creator. So He who made the oath with Himself.

> For when God made the promise to Abraham,
> He swore [an oath] by Himself, since He had no
> one greater by whom to swear. (Hebrews 6:13
> AMP)

Several scriptures describe the biblical covenant Yahovah had with Israel and thereby with us today. Yeshua gave us a new and better, an everlasting New Covenant in His own blood, not bulls, goats, or birds.

> Know therefore that Yahovah your Elohim is God, the faithful God who keeps covenant and steadfast love with those who love Him and keep His commandments, to a thousand generations. (Deuteronomy 7:9 KJV)

> But the steadfast love of Yahovah is from everlasting to everlasting on those who fear Him, and His righteousness to children's children, to those who *keep His covenant and remember to do His commandments.* (Psalm 103:17–18 KJV)

Jeremiah 31 speaks of the New Covenant with the house of Israel:

> I will be their Elohim, and they shall be my people. Behold, the days are coming, declares Yahovah, when I will make a new covenant with the house of Israel and the house of Judah, not like the covenant that I made with their fathers on the day when I took them by the hand to bring them out of the land of Egypt, my covenant that they broke, though I was their husband, declares Yahovah. But this is the covenant that I will make with the house of Israel after those days, declares Yahovah: I will put my law within them, and I will write it on their hearts. And I will be their Elohim, and they shall be my people. And no longer shall each one teach his neighbor and each his brother, saying, "Know Yahovah," for they shall all know me, from the least of them to the greatest, declares Yahovah. For I will forgive their

iniquity, and I will remember their sin no more.
(Jeremiah 31:33–34 NKJV)

Therefore He is the mediator of a New Covenant,
so that those who are called may receive the
promised eternal inheritance, since a death has
occurred that redeems them from the transgressions committed under the first covenant.
(Hebrew 9:15 NKJV)

Several significant covenants are given to us in the Scriptures.
Adam had a covenant, Noah had a covenant, and then Abraham had
a covenant. The children of Israel coming out of Egypt renewed the
covenant. Each covenant built upon the prior demands. Adam found
the reality of sin and the consequences of betrayal and treason. Noah,
righteous in his generation, built a boat, albeit a really big boat, to
rescue men based upon a promise still in the distant relationship with
God.

Not until the faith of Abram was a promise given to all nations
through one seed as promised in Genesis 3:15. Through the covenant with Abram, Yahovah told him his future generations would be
chosen priests and kings when as yet there were none of them. He
held to the promise.

I will put enmity between thee and the woman,
and between thy seed and her seed. It shall bruise
thy head and thou shalt bruise his heel. (Genesis
3:15)

Genesis 12:7 tells of conversation between the two covenant
parties. The promise/oath to Abram in Genesis 12:2–3 (NKJV),
*"And I will make of thee a great nation, and I will bless thee, and make
thy name great; and thou shalt be a blessing: And I will bless them that
bless thee, and curse him that curses thee: and in thee shall all families of
the earth be blessed."* This oath still stands today. As believers we are

children of the promise. We have the same blessings. They are ours *now*, today.

Yahovah changed the promise to a covenant in Genesis 15. After a personal conversation between the two parties, Yahovah declares the covenant to Abram. Starting in verse 9, Yahovah tells him to take a heifer, a goat, a ram, a turtledove, and a pigeon. Cut the animals in half and lay them and the whole birds on earth; Yahovah Elohim told Abram to go to take a nap and watch. Yahovah substituted or stood in for Abram. He passed between the bloody parts, swearing an oath with Himself, ratifying the covenant, in verse 17, a smoking furnace and burning lamp. Every sacrificial animal in Leviticus was included. "And it came to pass, that, when the sun went down, and it was dark, behold a smoking furnace, and a burning lamp that passed between those pieces. 18 In the same day Yahovah Elohim made a covenant with Abram, saying, unto thy seed have I given this land, from the river of Egypt unto the great river, the river Euphrates" (vv. 17–18).

Yahovah ratified the covenant with Himself. In KJV, it says in Genesis 15:18 to *make* the covenant, but in Hebrew, it states to *cut* (Strong's word 3772) the covenant or to firmly establish as an irrevocable covenant.

In Genesis 17, Yahovah restates the covenant by promising the covenant as generational forever, changing Abram's name to Abraham by adding part of Elohim—HM—the Creator's name to Abram's. There are no vowels in Hebrew when Yahovah Elohim takes a part of his own identification and added to Abram to make Abraham to strengthen his walk and faithfully declaring him to be a father of many nations, a kingdom of priests and kings.

> And I will establish my covenant between me
> and thee and thy seed after thee in their genera-
> tions for an everlasting covenant, to be a Elohim
> unto thee, and to thy seed after thee. And I will
> give unto thee, and to thy seed after thee, the
> land wherein thou art a stranger, all the land
> of Canaan, for an everlasting possession; and
> I will be their Elohim. And Elohim said unto

Abraham, Thou shalt keep my covenant therefore, thou, and thy seed after thee in their generations. (Genesis 17:7–9 KJV)

Again the future covenant we now live is in Jeremiah 31:31–34 (KJV).

Behold, the days come, says Yahovah, that I will make a new covenant with the house of Israel, and with the house of Judah: Not according to the covenant that I made with their fathers in the day that I took them by the hand to bring them out of the land of Egypt; which my covenant they brake, although I was an husband (Master) unto them, says Yahovah: But this shall be the covenant that I will make with the house of Israel; After those days, says Yahovah, I will put my law in their inward parts, and write it in their hearts; and will be their Elohim, and they shall be my people. And they shall teach no more every man his neighbor, and every man his brother, saying, Know Yahovah: for they shall all know me, from the least of them unto the greatest of them, says Yahovah: for I will forgive their iniquity, and I will remember their sin no more.

We today are part of that covenant. Isaiah 56:3–8 tells us if we worship Yahovah and keep his commandments, we are gathered to His kingdom as children of the promise when we grab ahold of the covenant, keep the Sabbath, and worship the King as stated in Isaiah 56:3–8 (KJV).

Neither let the son of the stranger, that hath joined himself to Yahovah speak saying, Yahovah hath utterly separated me from His people neither let the eunuch say behold I'm a dry tree For thus says Yahovah unto the eunuchs that keep my Sabbaths, and choose the things that please me, and take hold of my covenant; Even unto them will I give in mine house and within my walls a place and a name better than of sons and of daughters: I will give them an everlasting name, that shall not be cut off. Also the sons of the stranger, that join themselves to Yahovah, to serve him, and to love the name of Yahovah, to be His servants, every one that keeps the Sabbath from polluting it, and taketh hold of my covenant; Even them will I bring to my holy mountain, and make them joyful in my house of prayer: their burnt offerings and their sacrifices shall be accepted upon mine altar; for mine house shall be called an house of prayer for all people. Yahovah Elohim, which gathers the outcasts of Israel says, Yet will I gather others to him, beside those that are gathered unto him. (Genesis 17:7–9 KJV)

There are many scriptures representing the covenant, but we Westerners are not taught the value of keeping covenant. Henry Stanley was commissioned to find Dr. David Livingston in Africa when Livingston does not reappear for several months. In the process, Stanley used blood covenants with several tribes to make his way through the jungle. According to legend, there were over fifty scars proving the covenants worth which started with trading a goat for a spear. That spear was the chief's specially bound and marked possession in the hands of a white man giving it all the power and authority of the whole tribe's support. He continued traveling through ever more hostile territory including head hunters making covenants until he finally found Livingston alive. The visual scars and the spear held all the evidence the hostile tribes needed to back off. No one broke the covenant on the oath of death. Covenants are just as real in the jungle of Africa as they are in the Bible and today.

Biblical covenants were established with animal sacrifices in the Old Covenant. Yeshua established the New Covenant. According to Matthew 5:17 (KJV), *"Think not that I am come to destroy the law, or the prophets: I am not come to destroy, but to fulfill."*

> The law and the prophets were until John: since that time the kingdom of God is preached, and every man presses into it. And it is easier for heaven and earth to pass, than one tittle of the law to fail. (Luke 16:16–17 KJV)

Yeshua did not annul the Old Covenant with its many commandments, Torah, laws; statutes were fulfilled—made known and understood; He ratified a new and better covenant by His own blood. He walked through the streets of Jerusalem in His own blood every step of the long trek up Golgotha's hill. There He died on a cruel cross destroying all our sins; after which He enters the Holy of Holies in heaven, placed His own blood on the atonement cover, then sat down at the right hand of the Father.

> Do not think that I came to do away with or undo the Law [of Moses] or the [writings of the] Prophets; I did not come to destroy but to fulfill. For I assure you and most solemnly say to you, until heaven and earth pass away, not the smallest letter or stroke [of the pen] will pass from the Law until all things [which it foreshadows] are accomplished. So whoever breaks one of the least [important] of these commandments, and teaches others to do the same, will be called least [important] in the kingdom of heaven; but whoever practices and teaches them, He will be called great in the kingdom of heaven. "For I say to you that unless your righteousness (uprightness, moral essence) is more than that of the scribes

and Pharisees, you will never enter the kingdom of heaven." (Matthew 5:17–20 AMP)

Sadly the words *New Testament* do not give us the connation of the New Covenant. This New Covenant is not like the original covenant as the priests had to enter the Holy of Holies every year and place the blood on the atonement cover. The blood only atoned for the sins of Israel, but the New Covenant is totally different; sins are removed not just covered.

As far as the east is from the west, So far has He removed our transgressions from us. (Psalm 103:12 NKJV)

Christ hath redeemed us from the curse of the law, being made a curse for us: for it is written, Cursed is every one that hangs on a tree. (Galatians 3:13 KJV)

For He hath made Him to be sin for us, who knew no sin; that we might be made the righteousness of God in Him. (1 Corinthians 5:21 KJV)

In whom we have redemption through His blood, the forgiveness of sins, according to the riches of His grace. (Ephesians 1:7 KJV)

And you, being dead in your sins and the uncircumcision of your flesh, hath he quickened together with him, having forgiven you all trespasses; Blotting out the handwriting of ordinances that was against us, which was contrary to us, and took it out of the way, nailing it to His cross; And having spoiled principalities and powers, he made a shew of them openly, triumphing over them in it. (Colossians 2:13–15 KJV)

The handwriting of ordinances against us, that certainly sounds like the court's verdict of not guilty—deleted warrant.

Colossians 3 says He deleted or eliminated our sins. The accuser would have no grounds for accusations if believers could just understand that one concept. "*That's how you once behaved, characterized by your evil deeds. But now it's time to eliminate them from your lives once and for all—anger, fits of rage, all forms of hatred, cursing, filthy speech, and lying. Lay aside your old Adam-self with its masquerade and disguise*" (Colossians 3:7–9 TPT).

The author of Hebrews quotes Jeremiah 31:31–34 in Hebrews 10:16,

> This is the covenant that I will make with them after those days, says Yahovah, I will put my laws into their hearts, and in their minds will I write them; And their *sins and iniquities will I remember no more*. Now where remission of these is, there is no more offering for sin. Having therefore, brethren, boldness to enter into the holiest by the blood of Yeshua, By a new and living way, which He hath consecrated for us, through the veil, that is to say, His flesh; And having an high priest over the house of Yahovah; Let us draw near with a true heart in full assurance of faith, having our hearts sprinkled from an evil conscience, and our bodies washed with pure water.

It bears repeating, "All their sins and iniquities will I remember no more." Yeshua's blood ratified the New Covenant, changing *cover to remove*, East from the West buried in the deepest sea, no longer able to remember, deleted.

Just as Yahovah *cut* the covenant with Abram by walking between the bloody parts of bull, goat, and lamb as a smoking furnace and a burning lamp in Genesis 15:17. The New Covenant was *cut* through Yeshua's blood, an irrevocable, unchangeable, everlasting oath covenant as He walked through the blood pouring from His body. He hung on a cruel cross and declared for all to hear, "It is finished."

It was a declaration of victory over the war the accuser only understood the ramifications three days later when the Redeemer rose from that grave victorious over death, hell, and the grave. The final war was won. Satan thought he had defeated God's plan by sacrificing the one he knew had healed the sick, raised the dead, gave back sight, healed the lepers, and cast out every demon sent to destroy the man Yeshua. They identified Him. They called Him by name. They knew who He was all along but thought death would be His end until…

> But we speak the wisdom of God in a mystery, the hidden wisdom which God ordained before the ages for our glory, which none of the rulers of this age knew; for had they known, they would not have crucified the Lord of glory. But as it is written: "Eye has not seen, nor ear heard, Nor have entered into the heart of man the things which God has prepared for those who love Him." But God has revealed them to us through His Spirit. For the Spirit searches all things, yes, the deep things of God. (1 Corinthians 2:7–10 KJV)

Spiritual war was declared destroying the works of the adversary through the many tools of the covenant. It was a skirmish before, now the adversary retaliate outright war against any of the believers who dare to belong to the King of kings. This is not a veiled covenant of words on a tablet rock or a scroll page but written in blood, Yeshua's blood.

As the Lamb of God became the Redeemer giving the Father His eternal family written in His Book of Life, we are set free to use the tools of faith; but we *must* use them and believe we have the answers before we even ask as promised. We can use the powerful Word of God as a weapon or spiritual tool of our faith like a physical sword in the spirit realm toward the adversary.

> Where do wars and fights come from among you? Do they not come from your desires for pleasure that war in your members? You lust and do not have. You murder and covet and cannot obtain. You fight and war. *Yet you do not have because you do not ask. You ask and do not receive, because you ask amiss*, that you may spend it on your pleasures. (James 4:1–3 KJV)

> They shall not labor in vain, Nor bring forth children for trouble; For they shall be the descendants of the blessed of Yahovah, And their offspring with them. "It shall come to pass That before they call, I will answer; And while they are still speaking, I will hear." (Isaiah 65:23–24 KJV)

> But thou, when thou pray enter into thy closet, and when thou hast shut thy door, pray to thy Father which is in secret; and thy Father which sees in secret shall reward thee openly. But when ye pray, use not vain repetitions, as the heathen do: for they think that they shall be heard for their much speaking. Be not ye therefore like unto them: for your Father knows what things ye have need of, before ye ask Him. (Matthew 6:6–8 KJV)

Intercessory prayer is a mighty tool many ignore maybe because they do not know what to pray for or how to pray. Prayer is a two-way conversation. We can worship, petition, ask, but we also must listen, confirm the answer, then act on the Word. It is not a time to watch but to participate in the relationship. When one knows they are loved and heard, the relationship becomes intimate as any in the physical. Expect to hear, expect an answer, part of covenant is two-way acceptance of the terms. It is the major method of spiritual warfare. Talking to God should not be any harder than talking to your child, husband, or neighbor. God's ears are always open to hear one of His beloved children's voices call Him Abba.

Books of Remembrance

When we approach the bench of the courts of heaven, we have no personal voice except forgiven. There are many Scripture using legal terms. Job, Ezekiel, Daniel, Isaiah, John, and Paul all had experiences in the courts of heaven.

Isaiah 1:18 KJV states, "*Come now, and let us reason together, Says Yahovah, though your sins are like scarlet, they shall be as white as snow; though they are red like crimson; they shall be as wool.*" Reason together has a legal implication, a transaction of huge magnitude that changes a life from crushed to complete, complete—fulfilled, He *in* us, we *in* Him and He *in* the Father who is one with the Holy Spirit.

> So when that day comes, you will know that I am
> living in the Father and that you are one with me,
> for I will be living in you. (John 14.20 KJV)

Job knew the significance of the court even when he himself had not attended. "*Now there was a day when the sons of God came to present themselves before Yahovah, and satan also came among them. And Yahovah said to satan, 'From where do you come?' So satan answered Yahovah and said, 'From going to and fro on the earth, and from walking back and forth on it*" (Job 1:6–7 KJV). In the thirtieth chapter of Job Yahovah's answer to his predicament while questioning everything stated by Job and his friends, I love when He asks Job a question, not expecting an answer but to put things in perspective. "Where were you when?" His final answer was a reversal of all that had happened when it was all restored in chapter 42. Satan knows our legal standing. He also knows his only legal position is when we open a door with our confession, behavior, or life experiences. He has a long memory.

Moses knew of the books as he states in Exodus 32:30–31 (NKJV). "*Yet now, if thou wilt forgive their sin; and if not, blot Me, I pray thee, out of thy book which thou hast written. And Yahovah said unto Moses, Whosoever hath sinned against Me, him will I blot out of my book*" (Job 1:6–7 KJV).

> Then those who feared Yahovah [with awe-filled reverence] spoke to one another; and Yahovah paid attention and heard it, and **a** *book of remembrance* was written before Him of those who fear Yahovah [with an attitude of reverence and respect] and who esteem His name. "They will be Mine," says Yahovah of hosts, "on that day when I publicly recognize them and openly declare them to be My own possession [that is, My very special treasure]. And I will have compassion on them and spare them as a man spares his own son who serves him." Then you will again distinguish between the righteous and the wicked, between the one who serves Elohim and the one who does not serve Him. (Malachi 3:16 AMP)

> A fiery stream issued and came forth from before Him. A thousand thousands ministered to Him; Ten thousand times ten thousand stood before Him. The court was seated, and the books were opened. (Daniel 7:10 KJV)

> And I saw the dead, small and great, standing before Yahovah, and books were opened. And another book was opened, which is the Book of Life. And the dead were judged according to their works, by the things which were written in the books. (Revelation 20:12 KJV)

The books of heaven are kept as record of our life. "*Your eyes saw my substance, being yet unformed. And in* Your book *they all were written, the days fashioned for me, when as yet there were none of them*" (Psalm 139:16 KJV). There is a personal book of remembrance from pre-birth to death. Second is the Lamb's Book of Life. As believers, we are in the Lamb's book. Those not written in this book have a different future.

COURTS OF HEAVEN

As I was praying one afternoon, I asked if I may enter the courts of heaven for a petition. It seemed the Holy Spirit opened a massive wooden door where I stood on the threshold for several minutes. I was amazed to be in the presence of the King. Like Esther, I was aware I could have been sent back without an answer, but love pulled me in. I stood beside a wooden table and ask for America. I was so deeply moved by our situation, all I could do was weep for her. I saw a massive Bima (Jewish for judgment seat) when I heard the declaration, "America shall be saved." I have stood on those words no matter what the media states or what the people around me try to tell me. I know what He said.

We have the right to enter the courts of heaven with a clean heart seeking answers of judgment, protection, healing, or anything that pertains to life and godliness. Entering the courts of heaven are different than our earthly courts, as the supreme judge is righteous, just, and full of compassion. There are protocols, special sessions with life-and-death decisions. Only these decisions do not have probation, suspensions, or prisons. Life is accounted for righteousness or not. You cannot bribe the court, nor can you fail to appear. There are more than one court agendas. Salvation decisions are brought to the court of grace. Other courts are for bloodline protection, as well as healing. You can come before the courts pleading for mercy or justice just as the woman who constantly approached the judge for justice.

In Luke 18:2–8 (KJV), Yeshua told them a parable, about how they should always pray and not give up.

"There was once a judge in a certain town," He said, "who didn't fear God, and didn't have any respect for people. There was a widow in that town, and she came to him and said, 'Judge my case! Vindicate me against my enemy!' For a long time he refused. But, in the end, he said to himself, 'It's true that I don't fear Elohim, and don't have any respect for people. But because this widow is causing me a lot of trouble, I will put her case right and vindicate her, so that she doesn't end up coming and giving me a black eye.' Well," said the master, "did you hear what this unjust judge says? And don't you think that Yahovah will see justice done for His chosen ones, who shout out to him day and night? Do you suppose he is deliberately delaying? Let me tell you, he will vindicate them very quickly. But when the Son of Man comes, will He find faith on the earth?" (Psalm 139:16 KJV)

Persistence with faith will bring the answer. Begging, crying, or bargaining with God will not bring the judgment one expects. Faith is the key. Ask in faith believing when you pray, not repeating ritualistically the same phrase over and over. Faith believes you already have the answer where hope has no foundation to hang on. Ephesians 6:13 says when you have done all you know to do, to *stand* on the scriptures.

"*Therefore, put on the complete armor of God, so that* you *will be able to [successfully] resist and* stand your ground *in the evil day [of danger], and having done everything [that the crisis demands], to stand firm [in your place, fully prepared, immovable, victorious]*" (Ephesians 6:13 AMP). State the truth of the Word, not the circumstances.

Isaiah 43.26 KJV states, "*Put Me in remembrance; Let us* contend *together; State your case that you may be acquitted.*" Remind Yahovah of His Word, the prophecy He gave you or the promise given to you from His Word.

Scripture has the answer.

> Then answered Yeshua and said unto them,
> Verily, verily, I say unto you, The Son can do
> nothing of Himself, but what He sees the Father
> do: for what things so ever He doeth, these also
> doeth the Son likewise. For the Father loves the
> Son, and shews Him all things that Himself
> doeth: and He will shew Him greater works than
> these, that ye may marvel. (John 5:19 KJV)

Yeshua set the pattern to know the Father's will. We can follow the example He set before us. What the Father says to the Son, the Son and the Holy Spirit says to us, and then we do.

I was thrilled as I listened to Robert Henderson's various teaching on the courts of heaven. I realized we all have the right to enter; we either do not want to or are afraid to enter the courts. Maybe we just don't know how. Yeshua's victory was legal triumph allowing us to enter the courts for legitimate transactions, petitions, and judgments. Worship and prayer will transport us to the throne room. As Henderson so aptly reminds us, make sure your own plate is clean before entering before the great judge of the earth. Never give the adversary reason to defeat your request by legal maneuvers of evil.

I have worked from job to job in the legal system. It can be intimidating. The courts of heaven are where we resolve our issues. Work through your problems and prepare yourself to enter His presence once again. Your heavenly Father waits to hear your voice once again.

THE WORD OF GOD

I will delight myself in Your statutes; I will not forget Your Word. (Psalm 119:16 NKJV)

God will uphold His Word above His name. The Word, according to Ephesians 6:17, is a sword, and Hebrews 4:12 says it is sharper than any two-edged sword which would cut as it is inserted and as it leaves the heart. Use the word as an attorney would use evidence in a court. *"For your promises are backed by all the honor of your name, literally, "you have exalted your word above all your name"* Psalms 138:2 (LB).

> Embrace the power of salvation's full deliverance, like a helmet to protect your thought from lies and take the mighty razor sharp Spirit-sword of the spoken Word of Elohim. (Ephesians 6:17–18 TPT)

> For the word of God is living and powerful, and sharper than any two-edged sword, piercing even to the division of soul and spirit, and of joints and marrow, and is a discerner of the thoughts and intents of the heart. (Hebrews 4:12 NKJV)

> Now faith is the assurance (title deed, confirmation) of things hoped for (divinely guaranteed), and the evidence of things not seen [the conviction of their reality—faith comprehends as fact what cannot be experienced by the physical

senses]. For by this [kind of] faith the men of old gained [divine] approval. (Hebrews 11:1–2 AMP)

Faith is not hope. "I hope I have…" Faith is the confident assurance based upon His Word; it is established in the spirit realm, even when the physical eye has not seen it manifested. Standing on that assurance brings the results. His Word does not change any more than God does.

> Bless and affectionately praise Yahovah, O my soul, And all that is [deep] within me, bless His holy name. Bless and affectionately praise Yahovah, O my soul, And do not forget any of His benefits. (Psalm 103:1–2 AMP)

The benefits of serving the Lord are all found in the Word of the living God. Search the Scriptures, stand on the Word, and don't let anyone or anything change your mind or confession.

The Word of God is our spiritual sword to defeat the enemy. We have spiritual armor we need to apply daily.

> In conclusion, be strong in the Lord [draw your strength from Him and be empowered through your union with Him] and in the power of His [boundless] might. Put on the *full armor of God* for His precepts are like the splendid armor of a heavily-armed soldier], so that you may be able to [successfully] stand up against all the schemes and the strategies and the deceits of the devil. For our struggle is not against flesh and blood [contending only with physical opponents], but against the rulers, against the powers, against the world forces of this [present] darkness, against the spiritual forces of wickedness in the heavenly (supernatural) places. Therefore, *put on the com-*

plete armor of God, so that you will be able to [successfully] resist and stand your ground in the evil day [of danger], and having done everything [that the crisis demands], to *stand firm* [in your place, fully prepared, immovable, victorious]. So stand firm and hold your ground, having tightened the wide *band of truth* (personal integrity, moral courage) around your waist and having put on the *breastplate of righteousness* (an upright heart), and having strapped on your feet the *gospel of peace* in preparation [to face the enemy with firm-footed stability and the readiness produced by the good news]. Above all, lift up the [protective] *shield of faith* with which you can extinguish all the flaming arrows of the evil one. And take the *helmet of salvation*, and the *sword of the Spirit, which is the Word of God.*

Pray for wisdom to understand the Word; walk in the vision God Himself had for us before our birth. When one refuses to release sin, forgiveness, bitterness, anger, or personal biases, we hold onto evil. There is only one method of redemption bringing peace in the presence of Yahovah and the relationship He created us to participate in. We need to examine our own lives before the Father to determine if we are exalting anything above the name of Yeshua that has become a god to us. When we allow *anything* to be between us, it becomes brokenness or a block to the relationship with our Creator as it was intended. We can examine these things, asking yourself what keeps you from the covenant blessings. Open your heart to the Great Physician for internal surgery to the experiences, thoughts, or behaviors destroying our portion of covenant blessings. Backtracking on the Word delays the answer. The spiritual battle continues for our souls.

I, even I, am He who blots out your transgressions for My own sake; And I will not remember

your sins. Put Me in remembrance; Let us contend together; State your case, that you may be
acquitted. (Isaiah 43:25–26, KJV)

Keep the Word in the front of the mind, not an afterthought. Remind God of His Word. Quote it, write it down; remember the prophecies given to you or the words spoken over your life pre-birth until now. I have heard more than one person thoughtfully exclaim, "Never thought of that for this situation." God is involved in *every* situation.

Casting down imaginations, and every high thing
that exalts itself against the knowledge of God,
and bringing into captivity every thought to the
obedience of Christ. (2 Corinthians 10:5 KJV)

Deuteronomy lists all the blessings promised to us and yet we walk in false humility, self-righteousness, and pride—not receiving what was already ours in the relationship. These are not just for Abraham and his seed but for us as children of the promise. We can claim them, walk in them, and be blessed as Abraham was.

And it shall come to pass, if thou shalt hearken
diligently unto the voice of Yahovah Elohim,
to observe and to do all His commandments
which I command thee this day, that Yahovah
Elohim will set thee on high above all nations
of the earth: And all these blessings shall come
on thee, and overtake thee, if thou shalt hearken unto the voice of Yahovah Elohim. Blessed
shalt thou be in the city, and blessed shalt thou
be in the field. Blessed shall be the fruit of thy
body, and the fruit of thy ground, and the fruit
of thy cattle, the increase of thy kine, and the
flocks of thy sheep. Blessed shall be thy basket
and thy store. Blessed shalt thou be when thou

come in, and blessed shalt thou be when thou go out. Yahovah shall cause thine enemies that rise up against thee to be smitten before thy face: they shall come out against thee one way, and flee before thee seven ways. Yahovah shall command the blessing upon thee in thy storehouses, and in all that thou set thine hand unto; and He shall bless thee in the land which Yahovah thy Elohim giveth thee. Yahovah shall establish thee an holy people unto Himself, as He hath sworn unto thee, if thou shalt keep the commandments of the Yahovah Elohim, and walk in His ways. And all people of the earth shall see that thou art called by the name of Yahovah; and they shall be afraid of thee. And Yahovah shall make thee plenteous in goods, in the fruit of thy body, and in the fruit of thy cattle, and in the fruit of thy ground, in the land which Yahovah swore unto thy fathers to give thee. Yahovah shall open unto thee His good treasure, the heaven to give the rain unto thy land in His season, and to bless all the work of thine hand: and thou shalt lend unto many nations, and thou shalt not borrow. And Yahovah shall make thee the head, and not the tail; and thou shalt be above only, and thou shalt not be beneath; if that thou hearken unto the commandments of the Yahovah Elohim, which I command thee this day, to observe and to do them: And thou shalt not go aside from any of the words which I command thee this day, to the right hand, or to the left, to go after other gods to serve them. (Deuteronomy 28:1–14 KJV)

Put your own name in this passage; see if it changes how you perceive the blessings available to you and your household. Believers need to repeat these verses in their prayers. Yahovah said to teach them to your children and to their children. I like the Amplified Bible:

> You shall teach them diligently to your children [impressing Elohim's precepts on their minds and penetrating their hearts with His truths] and shall speak of them when you sit in your house and when you walk on the road and when you lie down and when you get up. (Deuteronomy 6:7 AMP)

> Specially the day that thou stood before Yahovah thy Elohim in Horeb, when Yahovah said unto me, Gather me the people together, and I will make them hear my words, that they may learn to fear me all the days that they shall live upon the earth, and *that they may teach their children.* (Deuteronomy 4:10 KJV)

By accepting the cross's legal transaction and applying the covenant tools can the heart become filled with love and peace, filled with all the blessings of Ephesians 1:3–12 (NKJV).

> Blessed be the Elohim and Father of our Lord Yeshua the Christ, who has blessed us with every spiritual blessing in the heavenly places in Christ, just as He chose us in Him before the foundation of the world, that we should be holy and without blame before Him in love, having predestined us to adoption as sons by Yeshua Christ to Himself, according to the good pleasure of His will, to the praise of the glory of His grace, by which He made us accepted in the Beloved. In Him we have redemption through His blood, the forgiveness of sins, according to the riches of His grace which He made to abound toward us in all wisdom and

prudence, having made known to us the mystery of His will, according to His good pleasure which He purposed in Himself, that in the dispensation of the fullness of the times He might gather together in one all things in Christ, both which are in heaven and which are on earth—in Him. In Him also we have obtained an inheritance, being predestined according to the purpose of Him who works all things according to the counsel of His will, that we who first trusted in Christ should be to the praise of His glory.

Keep thy heart with all diligence; for out of it are the issues of life. (Proverbs 4:23 KJV)

Hear thou, my son, and be wise, and guide thine heart in the way. (Proverbs 23:19 KJV)

He that trusts in his own heart is a fool: but whoso walks wisely, he shall be delivered. (Proverbs 28:26 KJV)

Wisdom is the principal thing; therefore get wisdom: and with all thy getting get understanding. (Proverbs 4:7 KJV)

My son, let not them depart from thine eyes: keep sound wisdom and discretion. (Proverbs 3:21 KJV)

Our works cannot change our heart by doing what is good in your own eyes. We cannot earn or work for salvation. It is a free gift of God as in John 3:16 (NKJV), "For Elohim so loved the world that He gave His only begotten Son, that whoever believes in Him should not perish but have everlasting life." We have to guard our heart to maintain the right path.

THE NAME OF GOD

The study of the names of *God* would take a book itself. Names are important in the Old Covenant. Many times the name describes the character of the individual. In Hebrew Genesis 1:1, Elohim is used as His creative name. Genesis 2:4 His personal name Yahovah is used. In Exodus, Yahovah actually defines His own name in two different scriptures. In Exodus 3:14, while talking to Moses, He tells him *I am that I am* but continues on to explain what the definition of that name means in Hebrew: I am, I was, I shall be. All forms of the verb to be. Verse 12 Yahovah says, "*I will be with thee.*" This is the conjugation of "to be." The exact same words are used again in the fifteenth verse when Yahovah tells Moses, "I will be with thee," Yahovah Elohim of your fathers, the God (Elohim) of Abraham, Isaac, Jacob, this is my name forever. Ya (I am), Ho (I was), Vah (I will be). "*Yahovah* this is my memorial forever to all generations."

Exodus 34:5–7 (KJV) is His own name defined by Himself:

And Yahovah descended in the cloud, and stood with him there, and proclaimed the name Yahovah. And Yahovah passed by before him, and proclaimed, *Yahovah, Yahovah, Elohim, merciful and gracious, longsuffering, and abundant in goodness and truth, Keeping mercy for thousands, forgiving iniquity and transgression and sin, and that will by no means clear the guilty; visiting the iniquity of the fathers upon the children, and upon the children's children, unto the third and to the fourth generation.*

All these are Hebrew words defining Yahovah's attributes of abundant merciful love of the Creator. He loves people and is filled with grace, bearing mercy while forgiving, declaring the covenant to His chosen people. This same definition is repeated in seven other places: Joel 2:13; Jonah 4:2; Psalms 78:38, 86:15, 103:8; Nehemiah 9:17. To just say God is to deny who He represents Himself to be. Just saying, "I love God," does not define which God or who you serve. Yahovah is love, not just has love, and wants His children responding lovingly to Him.

The vowel points in Hebrew of the name of Yahovah are found in over two thousand different manuscripts from several different historical documents in Syrian, Paleo, and Hebrew writings. The first vowel full points in Hebrew are found in Genesis 2:4. Yahovah has not changed His name in over six thousand years. Any other pronouncement would be a profanation of His name.

Isaiah 52:5–6 (KJV) speaks of a time Yahovah's name was profaned, but in the end, all shall know His name.

> "Now therefore, what have I here," says Yahovah,
> "That My people are taken away for nothing?
> Those who rule over them make them wail," Says
> Yahovah, "And My name is blasphemed contin-
> ually every day. Therefore My people shall know
> My name; Therefore they shall know in that day
> That I am He who speaks: 'Behold, it is I.'"

Exodus 20:7 tells us to not use His name in vain or falsely. "Thou shalt not take the name Yahovah thy Elohim in vain; for Yahovah will not hold him guiltless that taketh His name in vain" (Exodus 20:7 KJV). Using Yahwah could be to profane His name. Yahovah's name is repeated 6,827 times in the Old Covenant. Yahwah is based upon a false premise of the vowel points not intended for Yahovah's name.

> And in very deed for this cause have I raised thee
> up, for to shew in thee my power; and that *my*
> *name may be declared* throughout all the earth.

A name we do not know cannot be declared, exalted or worshiped. (Exodus 9:16 KJV)

And in that day shall ye say, Praise Yahovah, call upon His name, declare His doings among the people, make mention that *His name is exalted.* (Isaiah 12:4 NKJV)

Give unto Yahovah the glory due unto His name; worship Yahovah in the beauty of holiness. (Psalm 29:2 NKJV)

For from the rising of the sun even unto the going down of the same my name shall be great among the Gentiles; and in every place incense shall be offered unto my name, and a pure offering: *for my name shall be great among the heathen, says Yahovah of hosts.* (Malachi 1:11 NKJV)

He *is Yahovah our Elohim*; His judgments are in all the earth. Be ye mindful always of His covenant; the word which He commanded to a thousand generations. (1 Chronicles 16:14–15 NKJV)

He always honors His covenant. "He is Yahovah our Elohim: His judgments are in all the earth. He hath remembered His covenant forever, the word which He commanded to a thousand generations" (Psalm 105:7–8 KJV).

Yah in Psalms is the poetic name of Yahovah. "Sing to God, sing praises to His name; Extol Him who rides on the clouds, By His name *Yah*, And rejoice before Him" (Psalm 68:4 KJV).

In Matthew 1:22–24 (KJV), the name of Yahovah in Hebrew also appears.

Now all this was done, that it might be fulfilled which was spoken of Yahovah by the prophet, saying Behold, a virgin shall be with child, and shall bring forth a son, and they shall call His name Emmanuel, which being interpreted is, Elohim with us. Then Joseph being raised from sleep did as the angel of Yahovah had bidden him, and took unto him his wife.

Psalms repeats several times to remember the name of Yahovah.

His work is honorable and glorious: and His righteousness endures forever. He hath made His wonderful works to be remembered: Yahovah is gracious and full of compassion. He hath given meat unto them that fear Him: he will ever be mindful of His covenant. He hath shewed His people the power of His works, that He may give them the heritage of the heathen. The works of His hands are verity and judgment; all His commandments are sure. They stand fast for ever and ever, and are done in truth and uprightness. He sent redemption unto His people: He hath commanded His covenant forever: *holy and reverend is His name*. The fear of Yahovah is the beginning of wisdom: a good understanding have all they that do His commandments: His praise endures forever. (Psalm 111:3–10 KJV)

He also remembers us, His children. "Can a woman forget her sucking child, that she should not have compassion on the son of her womb? Yea, they may forget, yet will I not forget thee. Behold, I have graven thee upon the palms of my hands; thy walls are continually before me" (Isaiah 49:15–16 KJV).

Yahovah is not slack concerning His promise, as some men count slackness; but is longsuffering to us-ward, not willing that any should perish, but that all should come to repentance. (2 Peter 3:9 NKJV)

The Scriptures list several names of Yahovah, by no means the full list:

- Yahovah-jireh: "*The Lord is my provider*" (Genesis 22:14).
- Yahovah-ropha "*The Lord is my healer*" (Exodus 15:26, Jeremiah 33:6, 1 Kings 18:30, Job 5:17–18, Psalm 103:3, Psalm 146:3).
- Yahovah-nissi: "*The Lord our banner*" (Exodus 17:15).
- Yahovah-shalom: "The *Lord gives peace*" (Judges 6:24).
- Yahovah-tsidkeneau: "*The Lord our righteousness*" (Jeremiah 23:6).
- Yahovah-raah: "*The Lord my shepherd*" (Psalm 23:1, shepherd; Ezekiel 34:11–15, companion; Jeremiah 3:12–16, pastors; Judges 14:20, friend; Exodus 33:11, friend).
- Yahovah Savot: "*Lord of host, angel armies*" (1 Samuel 1:3, Psalm 24:10, Isaiah 22:14, Jeremiah 2:19, Amos 4:13, Haggai 2:9, Zechariah 8:6, and Malachi 2:16).
- Yahovah-Shama: "*The Lord is present*" (Ezekiel 48:35, Exodus 33:14, Matthew 28:20, Hebrews 13:5, John 14:16–17, Romans 8:9).
- Yahovah-InKaddesh: "The *Lord which sanctifies*" (Leviticus 20:7–8, 21:15, 21:23, 22:9, 22:16).

These area only a few of the compound names of God (*El* plus a descriptive word):

- El-shaddai: "*The Almighty God*" (Genesis 17:1, 28:3, 35:11; Ruth 1:20–21; Ruth 31 in Job; Ezekiel 10:5).
- El-elyon: "The *Most High God*" (Genesis 14:19, 22; Deuteronomy 32:8; Isaiah 14:1; Possessor of heaven and earth; Genesis 14:19, 22; Deuteronomy 32:8; Isaiah 14:14, Daniel 3:26, 4:17; Psalm 56:2).

- El-gib-bor: "*Mighty God*" over twenty verses (Psalm 147:5, Job 9:4, Job 26:14, Zephaniah 3:17, Psalm 62:11, Psalm 145:3, plus many more).
- Elohim: (Genesis 1:1; Matthew 22:44; Luke 19:31, 33, 34; Matthew 12:8; John 13:13; Matthew 6:24; Revelation 17:14).

We are valuable to God.

> But if the wicked will turn from all his sins that he hath committed, and keep all my statutes, and do that which is lawful and right, he shall surely live, he shall not die. All his transgressions that he hath committed, they shall not be mentioned unto Him: in his righteousness that he hath done he shall live. Have I any pleasure at all that the wicked should die? Says Yahovah Elohim: and not that he should return from his ways, and live? But when the righteous turns away from his righteousness, and commits iniquity, and doeth according to all the abominations that the wicked man doeth, shall he live? All his righteousness that he hath done shall not be mentioned: in his trespass that he hath trespassed, and in his sin that he hath sinned, in them shall he die. (Ezekiel 18:21–24 KJV)

It is disturbing, the name we should always remember has been removed, forgotten, and even maligned because of a false belief in man's ability to honor and revere the powerful holy name of our Creator.

When Yeshua said His Father is in Him, He literally meant the Father's name was *in* Him. His name means Yahovah saves. Moses actually named the Messiah three thousand years before His birth. Moses named Joshua YaHoshua in Numbers 13:16 (KJV), "*These are the names of the men whom Moses sent to spy out the land; but Moses called Hoshea the son of Nun, Joshua [Yahovah is salvation].*" Yahovah saves.

In ancient biblical Hebrew, J was pronounced as a Y. Yeshua was the same name only changed through colloquial speech over time and shortened into today's version, Yeshua. Yeshua was a Jew. He spoke Hebrew or Aramaic as most Jewish families living in Galilee. Many of the New Covenant books and letters were written in Hebrew with Hebrew idioms and phrases not easily translated into another language. The Septuagint was written in Greek which gave Him a Greek name to fit the congregation in the Greek communities.

There is controversy over the translation of the Bible into Greek. In 336–323 BC, Alexander the Great conquered Jerusalem and the surrounding kingdoms. He commissioned high priest Eleazar to send six rabbinic elders from each tribe who were fluent in Greek and Hebrew to Jerusalem to translate the Hebrew Scriptures into Greek. Alexander's thinking was the "common man" needed to be able to read the Holy Word in his own language since the language of his day was Greek. Seventy-two elders arrived to a sumptuous dinner, then sequestered on an island to complete the translation. In exactly seventy-two days, they presented a copy of Torah (Pentateuch: Genesis, Exodus, Leviticus, Numbers, and Deuteronomy) which was read out loud to the whole assembly. Much later in 285–246 BC the rest of the Old Covenant was translated to complete the project.

Even with many mistakes, it was used by many secular Jews and later Christians alike as the infallible Word. The rabbis made a concerted effort to hide the true name of Yahovah by translating the name "the Lord." They did not protect the name but essentially removed it from usage causing many to struggle with God's true name. Their reasoning of the name became a secret among the high priests; Yahovah was too holy for the common man to use. The name was used *only* once a year on Yom Kippur as the high priest entered the Holy of Holies to cover the sins of Israel for another year. They knew the name, just refused to use it.

THE NAMES OF YESHUA

It was prophesied in Luke 1:31 (NKJV), "*Behold, you will conceive and give birth to a son, and you are to give Him the name Jesus*" (Hebrew *Yeshua*). Even before He was conceived, He was named by God Himself. His parents were Jews who lived in Galilee, one of the many areas of Israel continuing to speak Hebrew. All the disciples except Matthew were fishermen from the Galilee community. The book of Matthew was written in Hebrew as a copy of the book is still found today.

Latin became the public language after Rome contracted with the rabbis to defeat the Greeks ridding Israel of the ungodly influence and atmosphere. The persecution of the Romans was just as harsh to the point it was unlawful to even speak the name of Yahovah. Thus the Maccabean war ensued. The thought of a pig on the temple holy altar revolted the high priest and his family enough to predicate a war. Four hundred years are between Malachi and Matthew; the Maccabean Revolt smack dab in the middle. Eventually that's where we find Herod and the Herodians who usurped positions of authority. Herod became governor, then usurping kingship. He married the high priest's daughter after Roman soldiers killed her father. Her mother wanted to stay in the political arena. She signed a marriage contract with Herod's father proposing Herod to marry Maria when she turned seventeen. He immediately divorced his current wife, sent her and her children away, and waited for Maria's birthday. In a fit of rage of jealously, Herod had her and their sons beheaded though he maintained the position during Yeshua's birth.

The language of the ruling party had been Greek which changed to Latin after Rome conquered the Greeks. The Jews still maintained scriptural Hebrew as Paul demonstrated rising to speak all three languages. The name was translated from Hebrew, Yeshua, into Greek, Iesous or Jesus, or a by-form (a parallel and sometimes less important form of a word, stem, or formative element in a given language or dialect first known use of) Yahushua, and Latin, Iesus. His momma called Him Yeshua from Nazareth. Whichever name is used, Yeshua or Jesus, it is a name above *all* others.

> Let this mind be in you which was also in Messiah Yeshua, who, being in the form of Elohim, did not consider it robbery to be equal with Elohim, but made Himself of no reputation, taking the form of a bondservant, and coming in the likeness of men. And being found in appearance as a man, He humbled Himself and became obedient to the point of death, even the death of the cross. Therefore Yahovah also has highly exalted Him and given Him the name which is above every name, that at the name of Yeshua every knee should bow, of those in heaven, and of those on earth, and of those under the earth, and that every tongue should confess that Yeshua Messiah is Lord, to the glory of Yahovah the Father. (Philippians 2:5–11 KJV)

The name is above all others as stated by Paul in Philippians 2:9–11. Using the name of Yeshua could be called a tool, but it is a benefit of the covenant. The name gives us all authority because of what He died for. All of heaven and earth stands behind that name. Even satan has to bow to the authority of His name.

Covenant Rights and Benefits

We are blessed and have covenant rights and tools which have not changed in over four thousand years. It is high time the ecclesia fully understand the covenant Yeshua instituted with His own blood. When we take communion, we are reminded of the covenant rights we have in remembrance of Him. Not our will but the will of the Father is declared in the Lord's Prayer. Do we really believe, trust, and accept that if He lives in us, it is already ours? "*Thy kingdom come thy will be done on earth as it is in heaven*" (Matthew 6:10 KJV). There is no sickness, pain, or death in heaven.

While Yeshua was at table with the disciples, He tells us in John 14 a brief but powerful, conversation. Yeshua declared He works through the Father and would give you authority to do greater things. The full power of the Godhead: Father, Son, and Holy Spirit dwell in *you*. There is not mention of the upcoming death, suffering, or resurrection, only relationship with the Father.

> Do you not believe that I am in the Father, and the Father in Me? The words that I speak to you I do not speak on My own authority; but the Father who dwells in Me does the works. Believe Me that I am in the Father and the Father in Me, or else believe Me for the sake of the works themselves. Most assuredly, I say to you, he who believes in Me, the works that I do he will do also; and greater works than these he will do, because I go to My Father. And whatever you ask

in My name, that I will do, that the Father may
be glorified in the Son. If you ask anything in My
name, I will do it. (John 10:10–14 NKJV)

We walk in righteousness; we are filled, and we would become
something never before created, *new* as in non-existing before, not an
upgraded model or version but *new*. Now there are four of us in one.
Yeshua in the Father, the Father in the Son, the Holy Spirit witnessed
and taught and then us, the redeemed, walk in loving relationship,
all as one. God *in* us.

When I was a child growing up, my three brothers and I would
help our dad work on the cars, tractors, or big rig trucks. One or the
other always needed something from oil change to engine change. It
was up to us to gopher parts, wrenches, or whatever. Daddy used to
say, "There's a right tool for the job. Use the right tool." Sometimes
following up with "find me a hammer." As a believer, we have tools
to obtain our rights and benefits. Knowing we have rights is only the
beginning.

If we have a car and do not insert the key into the ignition
because we don't know how, we cannot drive where we need to go.
The same with the Word's answers, we have to access the teaching or
instruction by Holy Spirit. Spending time daily with our Savior gives
us the intimate relationship needed to fully understand how to use
the tools. Praying in agreement, binding and loosing, communion,
tithing, learning to love as He loved are only a few of the tools or
rights we have in our living covenant.

Reading the owner's manual gives all the incidental instructions,
how to turn on the wipers, the rear defrost, or the inside overhead
lights. The Word of God tells us how to access the power of Holy
Spirit, how to heat up your relationship with our Savior, as well as
how to use the tools of our faith.

COMMUNION

Communion has always been an anomaly to me. I know we do this in remembrance of Yeshua. What do we remember, His life, ministry, suffering, death, or His victory, or all of it? Do we do this once year, once a month, a week, or how often? There is no standard time set. Communion is a confession of faith in the finished work of the Messiah for us.

Several months ago, communion began to take on a whole new dimension. I was strongly impressed to begin taking communion every day. I only heard stories it was okay from other people. I was strongly impressed to do so. My body responded in multiple ways—energy level increased, my understanding of His Word opened up, relationship with the lover of my soul was significant.

I became obsessed with reading about the blood of Yeshua. I reread several books in my library: Charles Spurgen, Charles Finney, David Alsobrook, Benny Hinn, Malcom Smith, Andrew Murray, Richard Booker, and whole batch of others. I even ordered some new ones online. Then I read Beni Johnson's book *Power of the Blood*. What a revelation, communion daily and sometimes several times a day. I knew I was on the right track.

Communion is not just a ceremony we perform once a month but taking into our body the resurrected body and blood of our Redeemer. He is *in* us, and we are *in* Him as He is *in* the Father by the Holy Spirit. After taking communion and marveling over the cross, His suffering and the fact He said yes even from the foundation of the earth, I heard Yeshua tell me to let Him get down off the cross, remember the victory, not magnify the suffering. I was not crediting Him with the finished work. Without the victory over the death of the cross, we would have no victory, no healing in His name or salvation promising a future. My perception changed drastically. Daily calling a friend who joined in communion our prayers changed to victorious rejoicing and revelation knowledge. He *arose*; He is *not* on the cross. It was a method of purchasing our redemption, ratifying the New Covenant in His own blood. Now we walk in covenant relationship. There are forty verses dealing with communion. These are only a few:

> For as often as you eat this bread and drink the cup, you proclaim the Lord's death until He comes. (1 Corinthians 11:26 NKJV)

> And they devoted themselves to the apostles' teaching and the fellowship, to the breaking of bread and the prayers. (Acts 2:42 NKJV)

> The cup of blessing that we bless is it not a participation in the blood of Christ? The bread that we break is it not a participation in the body of Christ? 17 Because there is one bread, we who are many are one body, for we all partake of the one bread. (1 Corinthians 10:16 NKJV)

> For I received from Yahovah what I also delivered to you, that the Lord Yeshua on the night when He was betrayed took bread. And when He had given thanks, He broke it, and said, "This is my body which is for you. Do this in remembrance of me." (1 Corinthians 11:23 NKJV)

> In the same way also He took the cup, after supper, saying, "This cup is the new covenant in my blood. Do this, as often as you drink it, in remembrance of me." Whoever, therefore, eats the bread or drinks the cup of the Lord in an

unworthy manner will be guilty concerning the body and blood of the Lord. Let a person examine himself, then, and so eat of the bread and drink of the cup. That is why many of you are weak and ill, and some have died. (1 Corinthians 11:25–28, 30 NKJV)

But when we are judged by the Lord, we are disciplined so that we may not be condemned along with the world. (1 Corinthians 11:32 NKJV)

You cannot drink the cup of the Lord and the cup of demons; you cannot partake of the Lord's Table and of the table of demons. Or do we provoke the Lord to jealousy? Are we stronger than He? (1 Corinthians 11:21–22 NKJV)

We put on the armor of our faith; it is all on the outside. Communion is on the inside. It changes our DNA; it changes our relationship, changes to living in health. Love can only be explained by the relationship that has always been. Yahovah the Father, Yeshua the Son, and the Holy Spirit are all in absolute agreement, *one* in us. We were created with Adam to be face-to-face, cheek-to-cheek relationship with God. Love has never changed. Religion lies to us with rules, to-do lists, false concepts we have been taught about God. We have been taught that He is angry. We have to please Him somehow. We can't measure up. We're not enough; we don't have what it takes to talk to God, all lies. His love has never changed from the beginning.

His love has always been an extravagant, unending, explosive, unrelenting love affair with His creation. He did not create us to make us humble, weak, or bowed down with grief, fear, and unmet expectations. We don't have to prove our value to the Creator. He created us to enjoy and experience an explosive love relationship with Himself. He invited mankind to participate in the dance with Him, experience love at its fullest extent without end, without brokenness, without guilt or shame. Where has the church taken a left turn into self-righteousness, demanding works, have tos and must dos to be accepted with God?

All along, He accepted us, loved us, and wants us with all of His Father heart. We have always been cherished to Yahovah and His presence. We have not always accepted His invitation to relationship. He loves us not because of our sin but in spite of our sins. He is always waiting for opportunities for us to sit at His table of love.

One day, as I was at a therapy session, I heard the old song, "I want to dance with you." It seemed Yeshua's dance card was filled with me, and He was offering His hand for the dance of a life time.

TITHING

Tithing is seldom taught in many congregations. I once attended a church where the pastor stated tithe is one topic so personal it is not to be mentioned in a sermon. I'm sorry but hog wash! Tithing is essential for personal finances, giving to the widows and orphans, and keeping the lights on in the building. I recently heard a young man say he no longer needed to tithe in the New Covenant. I don't find a scripture for such; there is a scripture in Matthew 23:23 (AMP) Yeshua stated,

> Woe to you, [self-righteous] scribes and Pharisees, hypocrites! For you give a tenth (tithe) of your mint and dill and cumin [focusing on minor matters], and have neglected the weightier [more important moral and spiritual] provisions of the Law: justice and mercy and faithfulness; but these are the [primary] things you ought to have done without neglecting the others.

He said you ought to have done *without* neglecting the others.

> Honor Yahovah with your wealth And with the first fruits of all your crops (income); Then your barns will be abundantly filled And your vats will overflow with new wine. My son, do not reject or take lightly the discipline of Yahovah [learn from your mistakes and the testing that comes from

His correction through discipline]; Nor despise
His rebuke. (Proverbs 3:9–11 AMP)

"'The silver is Mine, and the gold is Mine,' says Yahovah of hosts"
((Haggai 2:8 NKJV). We are privileged and honored to use what He
gives us; it is all *his*.

> The priest, the son of Aaron, shall be with the
> Levites when they receive tithes, and they shall
> bring one-tenth of the tithes up to the house of our
> God, to the chambers of the storehouse. For the
> Israelites and the sons of Levi shall bring the offer-
> ing of the grain, the new wine, and the oil to the
> chambers; the utensils of the sanctuary, the priests
> who are ministering, the gatekeepers, and the sing-
> ers are there. *In this manner, we will not neglect the
> house of our God.* (Nehemiah 10:38–39 NKJV)

When Joseph ordered the Egyptians to pay a tax, it was twenty
percent. One-fifth of their income went to keep the government
alive.

> "Now that I have this day bought you and your
> land for Pharaoh, here is seed for you; sow the
> land. And at the harvests you shall give one-fifth
> to Pharaoh, and four-fifths shall be your own,
> as seed for the field and as food for yourselves
> and your households, and as food for your little
> ones." They said, "You have saved our lives; may
> it please my lord, we will be slaves to Pharaoh."
> So Joseph made it a statute concerning the land
> of Egypt and it stands to this day, that Pharaoh
> should have the fifth. (Genesis 43:23–26 NKJV)

Yahovah only suggests ten percent. The question always arises,
ten percent of what, the gross, the net, or is it split in different ways?

Those answers may be personal but according to Hebrew ten percent is of your increase.

Malachi 3:6–12 is repeating the blessing and promises of Deuteronomy 28:1–14 when He states we are promised blessings when we give.

> Now it shall come to pass, if you diligently obey the voice of Yahovah your God, to observe carefully all His commandments which I command you today, that Yahovah your God will set you high above all nations of the earth. And all these blessings shall come upon you and overtake you, because you obey the voice of Yahovah your God: "Blessed shall you be in the city, and blessed shall you be in the country. "Blessed shall be the fruit of your body, the produce of your ground and the increase of your herds, the increase of your cattle and the offspring of your flocks. "Blessed shall be your basket and your kneading bowl. "Blessed shall you be when you come in, and blessed shall you be when you go out. "Yahovah will cause your enemies who rise against you to be defeated before your face; they shall come out against you one way and flee before you seven ways. "Yahovah will command the blessing on you in your storehouses and in all to which you set your hand, and He will bless you in the land which Yahovah your God is giving you. "Yahovah will establish you as a holy people to Himself, just as He has sworn to you, if you keep the commandments of Yahovah your God and walk in His ways. Then all peoples of the earth shall see that you are called by the name of Yahovah, and they shall be afraid of you. And Yahovah will grant you plenty of goods, in the fruit of your body, in the increase of your livestock, and in the produce

of your ground, in the land of which Yahovah swore to your fathers to give you. Yahovah will open to you His good treasure, the heavens, to give the rain to your land in its season, and to bless all the work of your hand. You shall lend to many nations, but you shall not borrow. And Yahovah will make you the head and not the tail; you shall be above only, and not be beneath, if you heed the commandments of Yahovah your God, which I command you today, and are careful to observe them. So you shall not turn aside from any of the words which I command you this day, to the right or the left, to go after other gods to serve them. (NKJV)

Malachi 3:6–12 (NKJV) says we are robbing God of our tithes.

"I Yahovah do not change. So you, the descendants of Jacob, are not destroyed. Ever since the time of your ancestors you have turned away from my decrees and have not kept them. Return to me, and I will return to you," says Yahovah Almighty. "But you ask, 'How are we to return?' Will a mere mortal rob God? Yet you rob me. But you ask, 'How are we robbing you?' In tithes and offerings. You are *under a curse-your whole nation-because you are robbing me. Bring the whole tithe into the storehouse*, that there may be food in my house. Test me in this," says Yahovah Almighty, "and see if I will not throw open the floodgates of heaven and pour out so much blessing that there will not be room enough to store it. I will prevent pests from devouring your crops, and the vines in your fields will not drop their fruit before it is ripe," says Yahovah Almighty. "Then all the nations will call you blessed, for yours will be a delightful land," says Yahovah Almighty.

We have tithing rights according to Malachi. He says to *test Him or prove Him. Will He not pour out so much blessing there will not be room enough to store it?* We need to take Him at His Word.

Deuteronomy, Malachi, and Proverbs all prophesy God will pour out so much blessing you won't have room to contain it. Tithing is essential. Personally, the bills are always paid, the rent is paid, and groceries on the table. Many years ago, I quit tithing, and the bottom fell out of my finances. I always thought I couldn't afford to give God anything, slight problem. He owned it in first place and was only allowing me to live on the ninety percent. I quickly returned to tithing and giving.

Tithing and giving are two different elements. *Tithe* by definition is a tenth. Giving is according to the Word of the Lord in each situation. Be open to His voice to an amount; be sure it is His voice and not emotions telling you what to give or the smooth voice of a preacher.

PENTECOST

The good news of the gospel is *now*; it is not future, but now we can have that relationship. We are *in* Christ, who is *in* the Father and *in* the Holy Spirit, not when death suddenly takes us. Yeshua tried to explain this to the disciples, but none seemed to understand the relationship He offered until their eyes were opened on Pentecost.

Pentecost was a revelation the apostles were told to wait for. I'm sure they did not at that time fully understand the reason to wait or what would happen. They waited in unison in the anticipation of the presence of the King. Exactly five thousand years before the people were gathered together to build a tower to heaven. Religion took on the appearance of good; only the motivation behind was not worship but to discover God Himself. The court of heaven chose to divide the languages of the earth so they could not accomplish whatever they put their minds to.

Now five thousand years later, they sought God once again. The reversal of the tower of Babel suddenly shook the building as they all began to speak a language from heaven. They could hear it in the streets; they saw it in the flames of the Holy Spirit over their heads. The presence of a Holy Spirit showed up to prove His power and manifestation of His explosive love, using language once again, this time building a kingdom not of earthly dominion.

> And the whole earth was of one language, and
> of one speech. And it came to pass, as they jour-
> neyed from the east, that they found a plain in
> the land of Shinar; and they dwelt there. And
> they said one to another, Go to, let us make

brick, and burn them thoroughly. And they had brick for stone, and slime had they for mortar. And they said, Go to, let us build us a city and a tower, whose top may reach unto heaven; and let us make us a name, lest we be scattered abroad upon the face of the whole earth. And Yahovah came down to see the city and the tower, which the children of men built. And Yahovah said, Behold, the people is one, and they have all one language; and this they begin to do: and *now nothing will be restrained from them, which they have imagined to do*. Go to, let us go down, and there confound their language, that they may not understand one another's speech. So Yahovah scattered them abroad from thence upon the face of all the earth: and they left off building the city. Therefore is the name of it called Babel; because Yahovah did there confound the language of all the earth: and from thence did Yahovah scatter them abroad upon the face of all the earth. (Genesis 11:1–9 NKJV)

The repetition of Pentecost occurred after Yeshua rose when He told them to wait until they were endued with power as stated in Acts 2:1–13 (KJV).

And when the day of Pentecost was fully come, they were all with one accord in one place. And suddenly there came a sound from heaven as of a rushing mighty wind, and it filled the house where they were sitting. And there appeared unto them cloven tongues like as of fire, and it sat upon each of them. And they were all filled with the Holy Ghost, and began to speak with other tongues, as the Spirit gave them utterance. And there were dwelling at Jerusalem Jews, devout men, out of every nation under heaven. Now when this was noised abroad, the multitude came together, and was confounded, because that every *man heard them speak in his own language*. And they were all amazed and marveled, saying one to another, Behold, are not all these which speak Galileans? And how hear we every man in our own tongue, wherein we were born? Parthians, and Medes, and Elamites, and the dwellers in Mesopotamia, and in Judea, and Cappadocia, in Pontus, and Asia, Phrygia, and Pamphylia, in Egypt, and in the parts of Libya about Cyrene, and strangers of Rome, Jews and proselytes, Cretes and Arabians, we do hear them speak in our tongues the wonderful works of God. And they were all amazed, and were in doubt, saying one to another, what meaneth this? Others mocking said, these men are full of new wine.

Pentecost is a powerful tool that pulls together as in Acts 2 or separates as in Genesis 11. Holy Spirt is not necessarily ignored today. He just doesn't manifest where not welcomed. Today the power of Pentecost is still alive and well. Praying in the Spirit is a way for our prayers to be answered when we have absolutely no idea how to pray.

With all prayer and petition pray [with specific requests] at all times [on every occasion and in every season] in the Spirit, and with this in view, stay alert with all perseverance and petition [interceding in prayer] for all God's people. (Ephesians 6:18 AMP)

What is it then? I will pray with the spirit, and I will pray with the understanding also; I will sing with the spirit, and I will sing with the understanding also. (1 Corinthians 14:15 KJV)

I think the Amplified is better explanation: "Then what am I to do? I will pray with the spirit [by the Holy Spirit that is within me] and I will pray with the mind [using words I understand]; I will sing with the spirit [by the Holy Spirit that is within me] and I will sing with the mind [using words I understand]" (1 Corinthians 14:15 AMP).

Many have a fear of Holy Spirit. Is it necessary to speak in tongues? To many, the answer is *no*. The Holy Spirit tells us when and how to pray. Our limited knowledge of spiritual matters and the will of the Father requires an adventure into the Father's heart not always accessible though our own language. Personally I want to be as close to His heart as I possibly can. I want to hear His heart against my ear, hear His whisper of love and instruction. When He tells me He loves me, it's like a kiss from my king.

THE POWER OF THE SHOFAR

When I first heard a shofar blown, the sound sent a spiritual vibration from the top of my head to the souls of my feet. I had to have one for myself. There is an unseen power in the shofar. Joshua used the power of the shofar to bring down the whole city of Jericho.

Now Jericho was straightly shut up because of the children of Israel: none went out, and none came in. And Yahovah said unto Joshua, See, I have given into thine hand Jericho, and the king thereof, and the mighty men of valor And ye shall compass the city, all ye men of war, and go round about the city once. Thus shalt thou do six days and seven priests shall bear before the ark *seven trumpets of rams horns*: and the seventh day ye shall compass the city seven times, and the priests shall *blow with the trumpets*. And it shall come to pass, that when they make a *long blast with the ram's horn*, and when ye hear the *sound of the trumpet*, all the people shall shout with a great shout; and the wall of the city shall fall down flat, and the people shall ascend up every man straight before him. And Joshua the son of Nun called the priests, and said unto them, Take up the Ark of the Covenant, and let seven priests bear *seven trumpets of rams' horns* before the ark of Yahovah. And He said unto the people, Pass on, and compass the city, and let him that is armed pass on before the ark of Yahovah. And it came to pass, when Joshua had spoken unto the people, that the seven priests bearing the *seven trumpets of rams' horns* passed on before Yahovah, and *blew with the trumpets*: and the ark of the covenant of Yahovah followed them. And the armed men went before the priests that *blew with the trumpets*, and the re-reward came after the ark, the priests going on, and *blowing with the trumpets*. And Joshua had commanded the people, saying, Ye shall not shout, nor make any noise with your voice, neither shall any word proceed out of your mouth, until the day I bid you shout; then shall ye shout. So the ark of Yahovah compassed the city, going about it once: and they came into the camp, and lodged in the camp. And Joshua rose early in the morning, and the priests took up the ark of Yahovah. And seven priests bearing *seven trumpets of rams' horns* before the ark of Yahovah went on continually, and *blew with the trumpets*: and the armed men went before them; but the re-reward came after the ark of Yahovah, the priests going on, and *blowing with the trumpets*. And the second day they compassed the city once, and returned into the camp: so they did six days. And it came to pass on the seventh day that they rose early about the dawning of the day, and compassed the city after the same manner seven times: only on that day they compassed the city seven times. And it came to pass at the seventh time, when the priests *blew with the trumpets*, Joshua said unto the people, Shout; for Yahovah hath given you the city. And the city shall be accursed, even it, and all that are therein, to Yahovah: only Rahab the harlot shall live, she and all that are with her in the house, because she hid the messengers that we sent. And ye, in any wise keep yourselves from the accursed thing, lest ye make yourselves accursed, when ye take of the accursed thing, and make the camp of Israel a curse, and trouble it. But all the silver, and gold, and vessels of brass and iron, are consecrated unto Yahovah: they shall come into the treasury of Yahovah. So the people shouted when the priests *blew with the trumpets*: and it came to pass, when the people heard the *sound of the trumpet*, and the people shouted with a great shout, that the wall fell down flat, so that the people went up into the city, every man straight before him, and they took the city. (Joshua 6:1–20 KJV)

Every time the verses use the term *trumpets of rams' horns*, Hebrews uses the word *shofar* being a sound similar to a trumpet. The call to move or stop in the desert was with a particular pattern of shofar blasts—attention, move out, stop, call to worship, and time to be in the presence of Yahovah.

The children of Israel heard the shofar for the first time on Mount Sinai when the shofar blasted continuously announcing the presence of Yahovah Himself on the top of the mountain. There is a rabbinic teaching the ram's horn was the second horn from the sacrifice provided to Abraham on Mount Moriah. Abraham took one horn, and Yahovah took the other.

And it came to pass on the third day in the morning, that there were thunders and lightning and a thick cloud upon the mount, and the *voice of the trumpet exceeding loud*; so that all the people that was in the camp trembled. And Moses brought forth the people out of the camp to meet with God; and they stood at the nether part of the mount. And Mount Sinai was altogether on a smoke, because Yahovah descended upon it in fire: and the smoke thereof ascended as the smoke of a furnace, and the whole mount quaked greatly. And when the *voice of the trumpet sounded long and waxed louder and louder*, Moses spoke, and God answered him by a voice. And Yahovah came down upon Mount Sinai, on the top of the mount: and Yahovah called Moses up to the top of the mount; and Moses went up. (Exodus 19:16–20 KJV)

In a service several years ago, the speaker asked me to blow the shofar. I picked up my shofar and blew to which she prophesied what the shofar was speaking. The next time I blew the shofar, there was another shofar that came from the heavens. No one had another shofar in the room. Everyone heard the sound.

The First Letter to Corinthians 15:51–52 (KJV) shows the trumpet or shofar will once again be blown by Yahovah, "Behold, I shew you a mystery; we shall not all sleep, but we shall all be changed, 52 In a moment, in the twinkling of an eye, at the last *trump*: for the *trumpet* shall sound, and the dead shall be raised incorruptible, and we shall be changed."

For Yahovah Himself shall descend from heaven with a shout, with the voice of the archangel, and with the *trump* of Elohim: and the dead in Christ shall rise first. (1 Thessalonians 4:16 KJV)

And He shall send His angels with a *great sound of a trumpet*, and they shall gather together His elect from the four winds, from one end of heaven to the other. (Matthew 24:21 KJV)

John also wrote of the seven trumpets in Revelation 11 prefaced with the same atmosphere in Exodus when Yahovah came down to the earth in the presence of all Israel. When the trumpets or shofars are blown, things in the Spirit follow such as in Revelation 11:19

(KJV), "*And the temple of God was opened in heaven, and there was seen in His temple the ark of His testament: and there were lightning, and voices, and thundering, and an earthquake, and great hail.*"

What does the shofar stand for? Good question. Many don't realize the shofar is a symbol of you. The horn can be made from any kosher animal including a cow, a ram, antelope, or an ibis. The horns are removed from the animal. After it is cleaned by boiling, all the morrow is carefully removed. The tip is cut, and the shofar is sanded and shaped if necessary to its final form before setting on a shelf to dry for up to a year. The tip can be set to an individual mouth and the tune or C or G for example. Most are recognized as instruments for worship or service.

So how is a shofar like us? We are removed from our old life, made new. We may have to go through a lot of "hot water" to allow Holy Spirit to clean all the "stuff" from our hearts which may take some time. No one is perfect overnight. The removal from the animal changes its purpose. I believe when we are born again, Holy Spirit changes our purpose, our DNA, and our family line. We are now adopted into the line of David, the eternal line of the Lion of Judah, the line of our Creator. We are no longer the same as it states in 1 Corinthians we are a *new* creature, a never-before existed person—new DNA.

> What? Know ye not that your body is the temple of the Holy Ghost which is in you, which ye have of God, and ye are not your own? (1 Corinthians 6:19 NKJV)

> Therefore if any man be in Christ, he is a new creature: old things are passed away; behold, all things are become new. (1 Corinthians 5:17 KJV)

New creation, new DNA, new Father, and like the shofar a whole new purpose. The shofar is a spiritual tool and has several uses even today: worship, call to war, praise, up and move out, stop and camp, danger, Day of Atonement on Rosh Shaneah, anointing the king, and Solomon's announcement of dedication of the New Temple. Today the world's biggest supply of rams' horns for the Jewish new year comes from a tiny hole-in-the-wall in Tel Aviv. One of Israel's main competitors in the shofar business is China.

In 1969, Ron Gardiner, an archaeologist, dug a few feet from the original corner of the temple and found the very corner stone where the shofar was blown every Sabbath. The stone fell into the dirt as the Roman destroyed the temple mount in Jerusalem. It is possibly one of the first stones to fall as it had several feet of debris covering the stone. The engraved Hebrew words were still legible, "To the place of trumpeting to announce." From this position, the priest could be heard all through the valley. To blow the shofar is to be a messenger or crier of truth.

I believe the shofar is a powerful tool. I have been prompted to blow north, south, east, and west when a breakthrough was necessary. When emotionally bound by current events, the shofar blast settled the atmosphere. I asked a friend if she would like to go with me to blow the shofar around the city. We went to all sides of our community and blew the shofar. There was a definite difference in the air. Shofar is another tool in our arsenal of spiritual weapons.

WE ARE LOVED

Over and over, Paul tells us that we are accepted, loved, predestined, chosen, beloved, treasured, along with dozens of other descriptions of who we are *in* Christ. Just in Ephesians 1, there are over thirty portrayals of who we are *in* Him. We need to realize He is describing the relationship God has always intended for His children. We are *loved*, not as second-class citizens but as adopted children. Abba Father is our declaration.

> For ye have not received the spirit of bondage again to fear; but ye have received the Spirit of adoption, whereby we cry, Abba, Father. The Spirit itself bears witness with our spirit, that we are the children of God: and if children, heirs also, heirs of God and fellow heirs with Christ, if indeed we suffer with Him so that we may also be glorified with Him. (Romans 8:15–17 KJV)

> And if you belong to Christ, then you are Abraham's descendants, heirs according to promise. (Galatians 3:29 KJV)

> Blessed be the God and Father of our Lord Jesus Christ, who according to His great mercy has caused us to be born again to a living hope through the resurrection of Yeshua the Messiah from the dead, to obtain an inheritance which is imperishable and undefiled and will not fade

away, reserved in heaven for you, who are protected by the power of God through faith for a
salvation ready to be revealed in the last time.
(Peter 1:3–5 KJV)

We cannot lose our inheritance through Yeshua Ha Messiah. It
is guaranteed. We can walk away, but to be adopted into the family
of God means we have the inheritance as Abraham being a son of
promise.

One day, as I was praying, one of my fur babies, Benji, came
and sat next to me. First thing I know he is laying upside down leaning against me sound asleep. I felt like Yeshua said that is what I need
to do with Him, learn to lean against Him and let Him take all my
troubles and cares.

Casting all your cares [all your anxieties, all your
worries, and all your concerns, once and for all]
on Him, for He cares about you [with deepest
affection, and watches over you very carefully].
(1 Peter 5:7 AMP)

I love the old Blackwood Brother's song "Learning to Lean."
The chorus says it all: "Learning to lean, learning to lean, I'm learning to lean on Jesus. Finding more power than I've ever dreamed, I'm
learning to lean on Jesus." The Blackwood Brothers were struggling
with their music when Johnny Stallings wrote this song in a somber
afternoon. It became their theme song going to the top of the charts.
It won the Nashville's Dove Awards for song of the year in 1977.

It became one of my favorites as I was learning to lean, not just
hope or guess, but to actually lean on Yeshua for everything: finances,
emotional support, physical healing, as well as spiritual growth.
Learning to lean is a process and not an overnight accomplishment.
It has taken a lot of years to finally let go and let God be my covenant
partner in my assignments.

What does it mean to be loved by God? Redeemed, never alone!
I love the old hymn "No Never Alone, No Never Alone," penned by

Ludie D. Pickett written in 1897. The words express His presence. We are always comforted, healed, and delivered. As a Father, Yahovah draws us even closer in relationship with Him; as we pray, we sense His presence, feel His heart beat, hear His voice. Our prayers are a direct contact to the throne room of the King of kings and the covenant existing before time began.

"Leaning on Jesus; Leaning on Jesus; Leaning on the Everlasting Arms" is an awesome hymn speaking to our hearts to continue to lean and trust on the Savior. Elisha A. Hoffman (1839–1929) wrote the stanza, and Anthony J. Showalter (1858–1924) wrote the refrain.

One morning as I was preparing to open my computer at work I heard a voice, "I love that you love me." After I quit being stunned, I felt His presence. He desires our attention, our willing heart, but most of all, our love in return.

DISCOVER JUDAISM'S TRUTH

Moving to Oregon changed my life in several immediate ways. I no longer walked on personal egg shells. I was a believer but with kitten teeth. Lion teeth were still hidden in the sheath because I did not know how to apply the Word effectively. I knew the New Covenant, how to lead someone to salvation, but rarely had the spiritual strength or understanding to stand on the Word.

A friend introduced me to a Jewish rabbi. I had never heard anyone quote Scripture as she did and her prayers blew me away. *She* had faith that I longed for. I asked if she would be interested in holding a small Bible study in her home, which she did for months. That changed my life forever. Suddenly I had a mentor I could relate to, one I could sit with and discuss Scripture for hours. She was offered a church building where a messianic congregation grew from a handful of people to believers coming from Spokane and Seattle. We learned the Torah; but we also learned to worship, dance, and be in the presence of the King.

Lion of Judah Dancers and Ministry lasted for several years. A small group even traveled on an unbelievable trip to Malaysia to teach Jewish folk dance. Shortly after we returned, she was suddenly moved away with her husband.

I had already been introduced to a Hebrew linguist professor, and his wife who had been attending the congregation. He offered to meet in my home for the next twelve years. We were reading the Weekly Torah portion along with the weekly Prophet portion. Each week, every Jewish congregation on Sabbath will read a designated portion of the Torah, along with the Prophet portion every year.

During the dark Greek and Roman days, it was the only way they could keep the Torah alive. During the Maccabean wars, it became unlawful to even own a Torah scroll. The children would use a dreidel to remind them of the Scriptures. The Hebrew letters on the dreidel were *nun, hey, shin*, and *gimmel*. The letters stood for "A great miracle happened there," referring to the Maccabean return to the temple. Jewish families would be dragged out, burnt alive along with their scroll and home. Even then, the dreidel turned; whichever side it landed, the child quoted new scripture verse as they played the "gambling" game in the yard unbeknown to the soldiers what it represented. One way or another, the Torah has been kept alive.

I had attended Columbia Life School of Theology and had a bachelor's degree in theology, but I discovered it was almost always on the New Testament. I knew almost nothing of the Old Testament. I knew Genesis. In the beginning, God created the heavens and the earth and then kicked Adam and Eve out and the Abrahamic covenant, Exodus and the ten commandments, Leviticus where life is in the blood, Numbers (who reads all those names), Deuteronomy gives us the Abrahamic blessing. I could not tell you how Isaiah or Jeremiah even fit in the picture. The time line of events was extremely skewed. Since a child, I had heard all the Bible stories—Daniel and the lion's den, Joshua and the battle of Jericho, and Ruth who changed her heritage—but to find them in the Bible, I had no idea where the stories were.

Suddenly the scriptures in Matthew, Mark, Luke, and John came alive as I discovered where some of the things were quoted came from. It was exciting to find "love your neighbor" in Leviticus 19:18 (NJKV), *"You shall not take vengeance or bear a grudge against any of your people, but you shall love your neighbor as yourself: I am Yahovah."*

When I discovered Scriptures of the Old Covenant were quoted or paraphrased in the New Covenant, it confirmed to me they were based on the same truth; God is love and has never changed His mind about His children. Why the revelation of that connection is not taught in many churches is beyond my understanding.

Yeshua rarely said a new thing in His teaching. When I discovered the many scriptures He quoted, I began to look for them. The most quoted book was Isaiah, but the concepts of many stories were always there. His mother had to have a good understanding of the Torah.

I discovered the repositioning of the order may have been on purpose, the Septuagint, then when King James Bible as it was translated into English. It has been stated, "The common man just cannot understand the Bible." Rearranging the order of the books helps keep the confusion alive. The Old Covenant was separated into law, history, poetry, and prophecy. There were *no* consecutive time lines. Not until I found a website that actually listed the Jewish kings with their counterpart prophets could I actually understand history in the biblical content.

I imagine I was not the only one who has difficulty understanding how the Bible all fits together in history. While I was a temporary pastor at a small church, most had never read their Bible. Little else knew where the books of the Bible placement were in their own Bible. The table of contents was their first reference. I felt the Holy Spirit suggest each week, we would discuss a new book and major historical events in original order and how they relate in the time line of the children of Israel. Wow, what a difference that made. People were actually reading their Bibles and asking questions.

Fitting how many of the beloved characters related to the time line helped to understand how history fit together. We may struggle with our own national history how some historical figures impact today. It is the same concept with the Bible. It is an actual family history, how they worked together, warred together, loved and lost together. All of it is based upon love given, accepted, and thrown away, then eventually turned back around to be the truth that gives eternal life for all who believe and become part of that same family—God's extended family.

Praise and Worship

As I listened to my brother sing "It's Amazing What Praising Can Do," I realized what is missing in so many lives; praise has left the room. I listen thankfully as worship leader Roma Waterman praised and worshipped from her heart. She reminded me Psalms was given to us for a reason. Praise takes us into His presence faster than any word or message we can hear or preach. Real praise is not always a canned song but a song that emanates from Holy Spirit opening up the heart to praise the Redeemer; you might call it a love song to the master.

"O sing unto Yahovah a new song: sing unto Yahovah, all the earth" (Psalm 96:1 NKJV). We can break that down, a new song, a never-before-existed song, a fresh song from the heart. A song will restore the heart, heal the soul, and bring a person face-to-face with the love. A worship song will change the atmosphere of worship.

Worship will take you from your existing emotions, hurts, and worries to a place of peace and revelation. Worship will change you, cover you in the overflowing river of His love, cutting away your burdens, shifting the atmosphere. We are a tripart being that craves to worship our God with our whole being: body, soul, and spirit.

> Praise Yahovah. Sing to Yahovah a new song, is praise in the assembly of His faithful people. Let Israel rejoice in their Maker; let the people of Zion be glad in their King. Let them praise His name with dancing and make music to Him with tumbrel and harp. For Yahovah takes delight in His people; He crowns the humble with vic-

tory. Let His faithful people rejoice in this honor and sing for joy on their beds. May the praise of Elohim be in their mouths and a double-edged sword in their hands, to inflict vengeance on the nations and punishment on the peoples, to bind their kings with fetters, their nobles with shackles of iron, to carry out the sentence written against them—this is the glory of all His faithful people. Praise Yahovah. (Psalm 149:1–9 NKJV)

From Scripture, it seems that praise cuts the fetters. Yahovah loves it, and the people rejoice. It doesn't take an instrument or a professional but a heart moved to honor. We all have a voice to worship.

There is good music, and there is bad music. I remember reading many years ago of a missionary who traveled to South Africa. He was escorted to his destination by a local guide. He pulled a cassette out of his pocket and asked if he would like to hear his son's latest music. As the music wafted in the wind, the guide pulled the jeep to the side and jumped out shouting he did not need to listen to demons brought into his country by some white man, refusing to return to the jeep until it was destroyed.

Many of the old hymns were inspired during existing events, all emotionally based upon experiences of the heart. When the heart worships, Elohim hears the cry of His children from Egypt to South Africa to America. God *loves* music! David created many musical instruments while spending endless days watching the sheep on the hillsides of Israel. We have many of those same instruments in updated form today.

While in Malaysia, Lion of Judah Dancers taught Jewish folk dance. When the congregation was asked to stay after the morning service, anyone wanting to learn to dance could stay and gather around. We expected only the flag ministry, and a few worshippers would join in. Shock, the whole congregation from tiny babies to the elderly all circled around and filled the whole room. We demonstrated a simple worship routine, then split up into groups and led the congregation in worship by dance. Talk about awesome; we danced to "Holy, Holy, Holy Is the Lord." The whole roomed moved in unison. It was like being in the court of heaven dancing before the King.

One of the most mesmerizing events of my whole life was in Malaysia. As the music started in the back of the room, everyone turned around. A procession with shofars, violins, guitars, drums, horns, and flags all slowly proceeded down the wide aisle. In front of the massive procession was a huge ruby-red, three-foot bejeweled crown held on the shoulders of four regally dressed men. The procession ended with the crown center stage on the platform, musicians strategically seating across the stage. The pastor invited anyone with shofars to join in the worship. The most awesome sound ever to hit my ear was the blast of a hundred shofars blown in worship of the King.

> He who dwells in the secret place of the Most High shall abide under the shadow of the Almighty. I will say of the Lord, "He is my refuge and my fortress; My God, in Him I will trust." (Psalm 91:1–2 NKJV)

Have you ever watched your shadow? It does exactly what you do, which indicates if I am in the shelter of the Most High and resting in His shadow, I must be praising and worshipping the King, along with the angels and the heavenly court. We need to praise and worship, not wallow in hurt, worry, or unmet expectations. Do the opposite of what you feel instead of worry, peace instead of pain, and hurt healing. Praise through it all.

Praise, worship, or dance will change your atmosphere; but it will change your city and nation. A psalm of David. *"I call to you, Yahovah come quickly to me; hear me when I call to you. May my prayer be set before you like incense; may the lifting up of my hands be like the evening sacrifice. Set a guard over my mouth, Lord; keep watch over the door of my lips"* (Psalm 141:1–3 NKJV). Watching our words is the beginning of praise and a turnaround in the Spirit.

Over 250 times, *praise* is in the Bible with over 150 times in Psalms alone. Praise should be the normal, not an exception. We can sing, dance, shout, cry—all praise to the King.

> Let everything that has breathe, praise Yahovah.
> (Psalm 150:6 NKJV)

Praise replaces fear, worry, anxiety, and the unknown. Let praise be first. Praise will give you strength for the challenge. Let Judah go first; Judah means praise in Hebrew. Praise first!

> Whoso offers praise glorifies me: and to him that
> orders his conversation aright will I shew the sal-
> vation of God. (Psalm 50:23 KJV)

COVENANT AUTHORITY

> Thus says Yahovah, the Redeemer of Israel, and His Holy One, to him whom man despises, to him whom the nation abhors, to a servant of rulers, Kings shall see and arise, princes also shall worship, because of Yahovah that is faithful, and the Holy One of Israel, and He shall choose thee. Thus says Yahovah, in an acceptable time have I heard thee, and in a day of salvation have I helped thee: and I will preserve thee, and give thee for a covenant of the people, to establish the earth, to cause to inherit the desolate heritages. (Isaiah 49:7–8 KJV)

Our authority comes through the covenant established from the beginning. When our authority suddenly drops into our spirit, it is like a light switch is flipped on with one thousand power watts shinning into the heart. Our circumstances do *not* dictate our position in Christ. We *are* representatives of the most powerful Creator in the universe, not subhuman seeking a handout. Let that sink in! What He says, we say. What He does, we do. Isn't that what Yeshua said in John 5:19 (NKJV)?

> Then Yeshua answered and said to them, "Most assuredly, I say to you, the Son can do nothing of Himself, but what He sees the Father do; for whatever He does, the Son also does in like manner. For the Father loves the Son, and shows Him

all things that He Himself does; and He will show Him greater works than these, that you may marvel. For as the Father raises the dead and gives life to them, even so the Son gives life to whom He will. For the Father judges no one, but has committed all judgment to the Son, that all should honor the Son just as they honor the Father. He who does not honor the Son does not honor the Father who sent Him."

Satan is scared to death of what a real believer will do. He knows the power we possess; many church people do not. I have walked many unhealthy and downright scary paths. Many years ago, I had a dream I was sitting on a chair in a small dark square room with a large light beaming down on my head. Suddenly a large man came through the door, swiped my wallet from my lap, threw it on the floor and ground its contents into the dust, with his huge boots. He stood over me and said in very threatening voice, "That's who you are," and walked out the same door. For almost fifteen years, I believed the lie. When I finally recommitted my life totally to Yeshua, I had another dream. I was walking down a county road with a couple of ladies. We saw an overhead bridge ahead of us when suddenly something fell from the bridge. Everyone else walked on, but my curiosity was peaked. I ran to the bridge support where I found a wallet on the ground. Picking it up, carefully opening, I stared at the contents. It was my same black wallet from fifteen years ago. I had my identity back. The Lord was restoring my identity, the call on my life, but above all, our relationship. Knowing our identity in Christ is crucial to understanding the covenant relationship.

Trustingly I submitted to be hypnotized by my spouse over a period of months. I did not know the possible consequences of that choice. When suddenly he died, I discovered an obsession with dying. I struggled with the mind games, vicious thoughts suddenly swamping my mind with all types of ways to die. While seeking the Lord one day, I suddenly heard the words "vow of death." I had no idea what that was, but it hung around my mind for days. Unexpectedly, the thought came to mind about the hypnotism; I asked the Lord what had been planted in my mind. Prayer revealed along with an activation key word. There was a vow "if he died, I would die." Well, that got my attention! He had been gone for several months. Days on end, I continued to have painful headaches. I had migraines when I was younger. I surmised they might be reoccurring. An extremely long month of painful days and nights continued until I had a vision early one afternoon. I saw a large two-inch metal band around my head with a screw type latch that was getting tighter and tighter with each passing day. I found a pastor to agree with me who wouldn't think I was completely off my rocker. After much prayer, I heard a snap and the sudden release of the pain. Instant healing coursed through my brain.

It didn't stop there. The next day, I had an open vision of a massive being sitting on a high throne cursing and shouting at a minion on the floor, "You let her go!" The minion groveled at the base and began to tremble when he whined. "We didn't let her go. She, she prayed and said that awful name and that *other* stuff." The being began to rage uncontrollably and shouted at the minion. "Do you realize what she could do to our kingdom?" With a few more shouts of condemnation, the minion was sent off to eternal damnation for disobeying the being. I understood the authority of the believer in agreement as never before. We can use the blood of Yeshua in our prayers to break the hold of the adversary. Satan has trampled on our rights; it's about time we trample on his self-imposed authority.

"He that digs a pit shall fall into it; and whoso breaks a hedge, a serpent shall bite him" (Ecclesiastes 10:8 NKJV). I have heard many stories about a hedge of protection through applying a blood line around families, cars, or businesses are secure. There was a hedge of protection around Job discussed in the first chapter verse 10, "Hast not thou made a hedge about him and his house and about all that he hath on every side? Thou has blessed the work of his hand and his substance s increased in the land" (KJV).

I have heard from several different sources about the Stevens family while on ministry in Canada. When tormented about thoughts of his children's safety back home, he held a prayer meeting asking for a bloodline to be drawn around his land. A week later, he received a letter stating there were five rabid foxes lying dead at the edge of their property. The bloodline protected his land and children.

The adversary cannot remove the ancient blood line either. He has to respect what is applied by the believer. He knows the power of the blood. As in the case of Job, he acknowledged the hedge of protection. Only with permission was he allowed to even be in Job's presence. The same applies to us except we know whose blood is applied to our lives.

> Cursed be he that removes his neighbor's landmark. And all the people shall say, Amen. (Deuteronomy 27:17 KJV)

> Remove not the ancient landmark, which thy fathers have set. (Proverbs 22:28 KJV)

"Remove not the old landmark; and enter not into the fields of the fatherless" (Proverbs 23:10 KJV). We declare the boundary by the blood, even the enemy knows not to cross the boundaries set by the Father. The boundaries of the blood will stand for all generations.

Covenant rights bring us closer to the Redeemer of your soul, protecting us on all sides. We abide in the secret place in His heart. *"But now in Christ Jesus ye who sometimes were far off are made nigh by the blood of Christ"* (Ephesians 2:13 KJV). *"In righteousness shalt thou be established:* thou *shalt be far from oppression; for thou shalt not fear: and from terror; for it shall not come near thee"* (Isaiah 54:14 KJV). He is our protection.

> He that dwells in the secret place of the most High shall abide under the shadow of the Almighty. I will say of Yahovah, He is my refuge and my fortress: my Elohim; in Him will I trust. Surely he shall deliver thee from the snare of the fowler, and from the noisome pestilence. He shall cover thee with His feathers, and under His wings

shalt thou trust: His truth shall be thy shield and buckler. Thou shalt not be afraid for the terror by night; nor for the arrow that flies by day; nor for the pestilence that walks in darkness; nor for the destruction that wastes at noonday. A thousand shall fall at thy side, and ten thousand at thy right hand; but it shall not come nigh thee. Only with thine eyes shalt thou behold and see the reward of the wicked. Because thou hast made Yahovah, which is my refuge, even the most High, thy habitation; There shall no evil befall thee, neither shall any plague come nigh thy dwelling. For He shall give His angels charge over thee, to keep thee in all thy ways. They shall bear thee up in their hands, lest thou dash thy foot against a stone. Thou shalt tread upon the lion and adder: the young lion and the dragon shalt thou trample under feet. Because He hath set His love upon me, therefore will I deliver him: I will set him on high, because He hath known my name. He shall call upon me, and I will answer him: I will be with him in trouble; I will deliver him, and honor him. With long life will I satisfy him and shew him my salvation. (Psalm 91 KJV)

Yahovah has promised protection in every place, time, or event. The hedge of protection with the blood line keeps others out while keeping ourselves in freedom with limitations of safety. Breaking the hedge is breaking out of the bloodline. When the hedge is broken, we are under threat of spiritual attack which leads to physical stagnancy. Only those who are rooted and grounded in power of the blood will flourish. When we walk in the will of the Father, we are given spiritual weapons or tools, understanding and discernment. Our life is not our own but bought with a price. The path is "in the book." The *Bible* is our *b*asic *i*nstruction *b*efore *l*eaving *e*arth. It behooves us to search it out, struggling with self-doubt but walking by faith. Use the weapons of the Spirit, reading the Word, and praying, expecting an answer. How will we know what to pray if we don't research and apply the appropriate Scriptures to our own situation?

> For the weapons of our warfare are not carnal but mighty in God for pulling down strongholds, casting down arguments and every high thing that exalts itself against the knowledge of God, bringing every thought into captivity to the obedience of Christ, and being ready to punish all disobedience when your obedience is fulfilled. (1 Corinthians 10:4–7 KJV)

Find the appropriate Scripture for the challenge you are facing. Put it in your heart. Put it on your mirror, on our refrigerator. Have it in front of you at all times until it sinks into the depths of your heart and soul. Repeat often, then once again until you know that you know in your heart the promises are for you. Covenant authority belongs to the believer to claim, declare, and live a life of redemptive freedom. The blood line is your wall of protection within the Word.

The Prayer of Agreement

The prayer of agreement is another covenant tool or right available to the believer. *"Again I say unto you, That if two of you shall agree on earth as touching anything that they shall ask, it shall be done for them of my Father which is in heaven. For where two or three are gathered together in my name, there am I in the midst of them"* (Matthew 18:19–20 KJV).

The name of Yeshua is given all dominion and authority. In His name we pray, we seek healing, financial support, spiritual life. *"Then He called His twelve disciples together, and gave them power and authority over all devils, and to cure diseases"* (Luke 9:1 KJV).

God has never removed His promises from the believer. Dr. Keith Moore lists 101 scriptures on healing I read over and over to reinforce my faith. If God said it before, it is appropriate to believe it today. I heard an outspoken radio preacher telling his congregation healing was only for the disciples. Funny, I didn't hear the scripture attached to that doctrine. Man-made unbelief has filled some congregations to such an extent it is difficult to correlate the truth to the covenant Yeshua died for. Man says God can't; God says, "I will." Which do we want to believe?

> Howbeit in vain do they worship me teaching for doctrines the commandments of men. For laying aside the commandment of God, ye hold the tradition of men. (Mark 9:7–8 KJV)

Yeshua stated in Mark 7:6–13 (AMP),

> He replied, "Rightly did Isaiah prophesy about you hypocrites (play-actors, pretenders), as it is written [in Scripture], 'These people honor Me with their lips, But their heart is far from Me.' They worship Me in vain [their worship is meaningless and worthless, a pretense], Teaching the precepts of men as doctrines [giving their traditions equal weight with the Scriptures]. You disregard and neglect the commandment of Elohim, and cling [faithfully] to the tradition of men." He was also saying to them, "You are experts at setting aside and nullifying the commandment of Elohim in order to keep your [man-made] tradition and regulations. So you nullify the [authority of the] word of Yahovah [acting as if it did not apply] because of your tradition which you have handed down [through the elders]. And you do many things such as that." (Mark 9:7–8 KJV)

Paul stated in Colossians 2:8 (AMP),

> See to it that no one takes you captive through philosophy and empty deception [pseudo-intellectual babble], according to the tradition [and musings] of mere men, following the elementary principles of this world, rather than following [the truth—the teachings of] Christ.

When two or more are gathered together anywhere, the power of their prayers are exponentially increased. A childlike faith in the Word of the living God can stand in any situation. The body of Christ as a whole should be in agreement. Even with differences of experiences, one can agree on God's Word as truth. Praying together builds faith, confidence, and assurance in the Word. Home churches and prayer meetings are popping up all across the nation to strengthen communities in tough times.

HEALING

<blockquote>

And the inhabitant shall not say, I am sick: the people that dwell therein shall be forgiven their iniquity. (Isaiah 33:24 KJV)

</blockquote>

Healing is not a tool but a benefit or provision of the covenant. Literally hundreds of Scriptures speak of healing of the sick. Yeshua went about healing *all* who were sick, and *all* were delivered of evil spirits. Starting with Genesis, we can find scriptures on healing, supply, wealth, all our needs. Noah was healthy, just drunk. The first infirmity actually mentioned were Isaac's eyes being dim. Then in Egypt, Jacob became ill and called for Joseph. The Israelites came out of Egypt all healthy. "*He brought them forth also with silver and gold, and there was not one feeble person among their tribes*" (Psalm 105:37 KJV).

Now that was a covenant promise kept! The blood on the door brought deliverance from the land, slavery, and infirmities—no blind, no deaf, no broken bones, and no diseases from the Egyptian slavery. Talk about covenant fulfillment. NKJV states in Psalm 105:37, "*Then he led the Israelites out; they carried silver and gold, and all of them were healthy and strong.*"

<blockquote>

He said, "If you listen carefully to Yahovah your Elohim and do what is right in His eyes, if you pay attention to His commands and keep all His decrees, I will not bring on you any of the diseases I brought on the Egyptians, for I am Yahovah, who heals you." (Exodus 15:26 NKJV)

</blockquote>

Thy raiment waxed not old upon thee, neither did thy foot swell, these forty years. (Deuteronomy 8:4 KJV)

"And I have led you forty years in the wilderness: your clothes are not waxen old upon you, and thy shoe is not waxen old upon thy foot" (Deuteronomy 29:5 KJV). Yahovah's provision kept them with food as manna, clean clothes, health, hot and cold protection. A cloud by day protected them from the extreme heat of the desert while the cloud also protected them from the harsh cold at night.

"Elohim went ahead of them in a Pillar of Cloud during the day to guide them on the way, and at night in a Pillar of Fire to give them light; thus they could travel both day and night. The Pillar of Cloud by day and the Pillar of Fire by night never left the people" (Exodus 13:21–22 KJV). It is taught in Judaism that the cloud covered them on all six sides: north, south, east, and west, above, and beneath. This protected them from the many critters in the desert: snakes, spiders, vipers, vultures, and even the wandering marauder.

As long as they traveled, the cloud stayed with them. The only time it was lifted was when they sinned and vipers were allowed into the camp. They were bitten and had to look at the copper snake on the pole for healing or die. Even, then Yahovah proved a method of redemption by looking at the pole.

Then they journeyed from Mount Hor by the Way of the Red Sea, to go around the land of Edom; and the soul of the people became very discouraged on the way. And the people spoke against Elohim and against Moses: "Why have you brought us up out of Egypt to die in the wilderness? For there is no food and no water, and our soul loathes this worthless bread." So Yahovah sent fiery serpents among the people, and they bit the people; and many of the people of Israel died. Therefore the people came to Moses, and said, "We have sinned, for we have

spoken against Yahovah and against you; pray to
Yahovah that He take away the serpents from us."
So Moses prayed for the people. Yahovah said
to Moses, "Make a fiery serpent, and set it on a
pole; and it shall be that everyone who is bitten,
when he looks at it, shall live." So Moses made
a bronze serpent, and put it on a pole; and so
it was, if a serpent had bitten anyone, when he
looked at the bronze serpent, he lived. (Numbers
21:4–9 NKJV)

Sin produces its own consequences of sickness, early death, and
hardship. God *never* puts sickness on anyone. Another man-made
doctrine destroying the faith of believers are punishment by illness,
cancer, diabetes, or whatever the malady. It does *not* come from God.
The enemy comes to steal, kill, and destroy.

The thief comes only in order to steal and kill
and destroy. I came that they may have and enjoy
life, and have it in abundance [to the full, *till it
overflows*]. (John 10:10 AMP)

Now is the judgment of this world: now shall the
prince of this world be cast out. And I, if I be
lifted up from the earth, will draw all men unto
me. (John 12:31–32 KJV)

It's a slap in God's holy merciful character to think He would
make you ill. We need to read the 101 verses on healing where we
find God healed them *all*. It would be helpful to research Dr. Keith
Moore's marvelous list of 101 verses on his website. In the New
Covenant alone, there are over thirty-nine scriptures on healing. Acts
is filled with the disciples healing everywhere they went. If Yahovah,
the Father, is the same today as He was yesterday—and if He was
healing people back in the past in the Old Covenant days—then
this means that He can and will continue to heal today. This is why

divine healing is still for everyone in this day and age. The gift of healing did not stop after the first set of apostles left the scene. *It is Gods will to heal.*

Many have been taught to say, "If it be thy will to heal…" Those words are not in the Bible anywhere. The only time Paul use "if it be the will of Lord" is when he mentions visiting one of the cities he has evangelized. Yeshua used the words by your faith, you are made whole or healed as the centurion's son, the widow's issue of blood or ten lepers.

> And Jesus said unto the centurion, Go thy way; and *as thou hast believed, so be it done unto thee.* And His servant was healed in the selfsame hour. (Matthew 10:52 KJV)

> And He said unto her, Daughter, *thy faith hath made thee whole*; go in peace, and be whole of thy plague. (Mark 5:34 KJV)

> And Jesus answering said, Were there not ten cleansed? but where are the nine? There are not found that returned to give glory to God, save this stranger. And He said unto him, Arise, go thy way: thy faith hath made thee whole. (Luke 10:17–19 KJV)

When we open a door by our confession or experiences, the adversary has good ears and will jump on your mental acquisition of a sickness, disease, or habit. Any opportunity to bring adverse effects upon the children of God, the antagonist already has a strategy in place hoping the believer will unintentionally succumb to his suggestion. We need to watch our confession, pray the Word, and expect it to be done.

> For verily I say unto you, That whosoever shall say unto this mountain, Be thou removed, and be

thou cast into the sea; and shall not doubt in his heart, but shall believe that those things which he says shall come to pass; he shall have whatsoever he says. Therefore I say unto you, what things so ever ye desire, when ye pray, believe that ye receive them, and ye shall have them. (Mark 11:23–24 KJV)

Speak faith to the mountain. Command the mountain to move.

John G. Lake, arguably the most famous of faith healers, told the hospital administrators in South Africa when a plague was killing thousands, to place a drop of the plague on his hand and watch it die. He volunteered to bury the dead as no one else would even touch a dead body. They watched in the microscope as the plague literally burned up and died on his hand.

Healing is still an application solely dependent upon God. Our faith activates a response. Even though some seem not to be healed here, only in heaven, it is still a mystery. I know many of faith with unanswered questions. I know our faith makes us whole. Standing on the Scriptures is the major key. There may be a key I am missing. I have seen the dead raised, bodies restored, and health reclaimed. I still don't know what the determining factor is. It is God's will to heal, after that faith. He has healed my body so many times I cannot count, but I see faith-filled believers still suffering; satan has misguided the body into believing God does not heal every time. I declare that to be a lie. God's will is to heal; our will is to stand on the Word.

KEYS OF THE KINGDOM

Another covenant tool or right seldom understood are the keys of the Kingdom of Heaven given to Peter in Matthew 16:19. They were given to all the body of Christ for kingdom authority for the whole ecclesia. The keys of the kingdom are not taught or understood in many churches based upon a false premise they were given only to Peter. Not so. It comes from Isaiah 22:22 (KJV) *"And the key of the house of David will I lay upon his shoulder; so he shall open, and none shall shut; and he shall shut, and none shall open."*

> And I will give unto thee the keys of the kingdom of heaven: and whatsoever thou shalt bind on earth shall be bound in heaven: and whatsoever thou shalt loose on earth shall be loosed in heaven. (Matthew 16:19 KJV)

The word *loose* in Matthew 16:19 is the Greek word *luo* defined as forbidden by an indisputable authority and to permit by an indisputable authority as Yeshua did on the cross. He destroyed (*luo*) the works of the devil. *Luo* means to void the contract, dissolve, or break the tie, or break into pieces that which bind, Strong's number 3089.

While speaking with a friend a few days ago, I suddenly realized she had never been taught on either concept of binding or loosing. Only through our relationship with our Savior, the heir of the house of David, can we use these keys. He *gave* us the keys for us to use.

"After this manner therefore pray ye: Our Father which art in heaven, Hallowed be thy name. Thy kingdom come, Thy will be done in earth, as it is in heaven" (Matthew 6:9 KJV). Thy will be done on

earth as it is in Heaven. The believer has the right to ask for the will in heaven to be on earth. Are we asking? He is *in* us. It is our privilege to ask heaven to be demonstrated here on earth, here and *now*. Opening doors only Holy Spirit can open, close those which need to be closed or are no longer needed, appropriate or healthy.

We know His will. We have sixty-six books to tell us His will. He has not changed, nor will He. When God said He *shall* perform His will to keep us, heal us, prosper us, save us, and protect us in the Old Covenant, then it definitely is His will in the New Covenant. My old pastor reminded often the definition of the word *shall* was "absolutely, positively, will without fail, come to pass," no room for doubt.

There are two separate teachings on binding and loosing. The believer can bind the enemy and loose peace by the blood of the lamb and the name of Yeshua. Then one can bind oneself to the will of the Father and loose the works of the past or religious to-do lists.

> And I also say to you that you are Peter, and on this rock I will build My church, and the gates of Hades shall not prevail against it. And I will give you the keys of the kingdom of heaven, and whatever you bind on earth will be bound in heaven, and whatever you loose on earth will be loosed in heaven. (Matthew 16:18–19 NKJV)

This is a struggle when one does not know the will of the Father for their lives. The Bible is God's will! Believers usually know when the adversary has physically attacked the mind or family. Spiritual attacks may not be as evident. Depression, oppression, anxiety, or fear may creep in before sudden realization of the depths of the battle. First, don't agree with the attack by words spoken from your own mouth causing an open door. These things are neither spiritual nor edifying. Recognize where they come from, bind them, release them, and *let* them to go. Accept and receive the deliverance, healing, and freedom from the Spirit.

No works will relieve the ambush. Distinguish between normal and attack. The spirit of discernment is given to the believer. Discernment of spirits distinguishes the good and the bad. Many declare through their own voice *my* depression, *my* sickness, or *my* fear of whatever. No, it is not yours. It is from the adversary. Sickness or disease is not a thing to enjoy or revel in as some do. Bind it, and let it loose. Receive freedom, liberty, and newness of life. Put on the new man. Isn't that what Ephesians and Colossians state? *"And that ye put on the new man, which after God is created in righteousness and true holiness"* (Ephesians 4:24 KJV).

> And have put on the new man, which is renewed in knowledge after the image of Him that created him. (Colossians 3:10 KJV)

> And do not be conformed to this world [any longer with its superficial values and customs], but be transformed and progressively changed [as you mature spiritually] by the renewing of your mind [focusing on godly values and ethical attitudes], so that you may prove [for yourselves] what the will of God is, that which is good and acceptable and perfect [in His plan and purpose for you]. (Romans 12:2 AMP)

> Therefore if anyone is in Christ [that is, grafted in, joined to Him by faith in Him as Savior], he is a new creature [reborn and renewed by the Holy Spirit]; the old things [the previous moral and spiritual condition] have passed away. Behold, new things have come [because spiritual awakening brings a new life]. (1 Corinthians 5:17 AMP)

We are not the same. Being born again is new life, a never existed before *you*—new life, new DNA, new Father, but most of all, a realization of the love that has been waiting for us to accept the sacrifice paid for our sins.

Let me state here, Yahovah has *always* loved us, but we have not always returned that love. He has always been there through thick and thin. I once ask where He was when I went through an extremely traumatic event. His response to me was He was there, but I refused His love trying to work things out on my own. No matter how hard the situation is, look around. You will find His arms open just as wide for you as the father of the prodigal son's welcoming you into His embrace.

The spirit of discernment is only one of the gifts of the Spirit which are discussed in the next chapter. Ask Yeshua what gifts are prevalent in your life. Some gifts are more prominent than others. A natural tendency toward a particular activity may indicate a gift such as singing, understanding strategy, or when to pray for a particular thing.

The keys of the kingdom are ours, but we need to access them. Just having the keys does not mean they are automatic to bring results. Knowing and using are two separate issues, binding and loosing, believing and declaring the truth as made evident by your understanding of the Word are essential, in heaven as on earth.

Gifts of the Spirit

Paul speaks of gifts given to the church for the edification of the believer. Spiritual gifts given by Holy Spirit give an orderly assembly leadership, along with different manifestations of His presence. *"And God has appointed these in the church: first apostles, second prophets, third teachers, after that miracles, then gifts of healings, helps, administrations, varieties of tongues"* (1 Corinthians 12:28 NKJV).

> Having then gifts differing according to the grace that is given to us, let us use them: if *prophecy*, let us prophesy in proportion to our faith; or ministry, let us use it in our ministering; he who *teaches*, in teaching; he who *exhorts*, in exhortation; he who *gives*, with liberality; he who *leads*, with diligence; he who shows *mercy*, with cheerfulness. (Romans 12:6–8 NKJV)

> But to each one of us grace was given according to the measure of Christ's gift. Therefore He says: "When He ascended on high, He led captivity captive, And *gave gifts to men.*" (Now this, "He ascended"—what does it mean but that He also first descended into the lower parts of the earth? He who descended is also the One who ascended far above all the heavens, that He might fill all things.) And He Himself gave some to be *apostles*, some *prophets*, some *evangelists*, and some *pastors and teachers*, for the equipping of the saints for

the work of ministry, for the edifying of the body
of Christ. (Ephesians 4:6–12 NKJV)

The Holy Spirit was sent by Yeshua, giving the church many spiritual gifts to understand how to live. Believers should pursue the gifts, not run from them as some teach. The gift of the Holy Spirit in 1 Corinthians quoted below is essential to the body and strengthens our spirit during challenges. There is only one Holy Spirit but many manifestations called gifts.

When I first became a believer many years ago, I was told all these gifts died when the disciples died. I didn't question that until I actually met some Spirit-filled tongue talkers for myself. They were no different than I was, not strange or weird. I ask a lot of questions. This was only the beginning, discovering there was a whole lot more to "spirit led" than I had been taught.

After being gloriously filled with the Holy Spirit, I was accosted by preachers and teachers alike, tell me it was not of God. There was a slight problem with their argument, no scriptural basis for their standing, only confusion of doctrine. They could not explain how all of a sudden, I seemed to have a better understanding of the Word, I felt more at peace, and the relationship with my Savior became more real.

I no longer question the availability of the gifts. The giver of the Spirit constantly teaches us as our inner man changes, develops, and finds new ways Holy Spirit leads. Most of the time, one manifestation will be stronger than another depending upon the unction from the Master which may change depending upon circumstances or needs of the Spirit.

I researched several commentaries, translations, and original Greek words concerning the definition of gifts as the word is used in all three scriptures. Strong's exhaustive Word study 5486 says "*charizomai*," gifts granted freely or given or bestowed willingly. There are different kinds of administration of the gifts. Paul's gifts were described as gifts of Holy Spirt freely given for diverse distribution.

The gift is without repentance. *"For the gifts and calling of God are without repentance"* Romans 11:29, KJV).

> A man's gift makes room for him, and brings him
> before great men. (Proverbs 18:16 KJV)

There is a purpose for each expression of Holy Spirit in edifying the church. We need to seek our gifting and ask the Holy Spirit to teach us how to be used, when to use the gift, and where. The Holy Spirit is a gentleman and does things decently and in order. We need to follow His leading, not lead Him or become a "junior Holy Spirit," thinking we know what is going in someone else's life.

> Now there are diversities of gifts, but the same Spirit. And there are differences of administrations, but the same Lord. And there are diversities of operations, but it is the same God which works all in all. But the manifestation of the Spirit is given to every man to profit withal. For to one is given by the *Spirit the word of wisdom*; to another the *word of knowledge* by the same Spirit; To another *faith by the same Spirit*; to another *the gifts of healing* by the same Spirit; To another the *working of miracles*; to another *prophecy*; to another *discerning of spirits*; to another *divers kinds of tongues;* to another *the interpretation of tongues*: But all these works that one and the selfsame Spirit, dividing to every man severally as He will. (1 Corinthians 12:4–11 KJV)

The Word of Wisdom may be demonstrated in new strategies not normally available or a new business or personal direction, not necessarily spiritual, but Holy Spirit will use it for the glory of the kingdom. Many Christian businesses are filled with God-given gifts to use their finances for the kingdom growth.

The word of knowledge may be when you have a word of knowl-edge about a situation or thing you did not have understanding before. When Kenneth Hagin spoke to a woman about forgiving a family member, Holy Spirit was giving him a word of knowledge. This could be an immediate word, dream, or idea bringing glory to God.

Gift of faith is sometimes confused with having faith in the beginning for salvation. This is manifested faith to believe for the impossible. I have heard the phrase "impossible is a word God never uses." If He gives us the desire, He will bring it to pass in His timing with or without our understanding of how, usually without!

The gifts of healing demonstrated every time John G. Lake, Oral Roberts, A. A. Allen, R. W. Schambach or Katheryn Kuhlman stepped on the platform. Documented healings were common only because they were willing to be used by Holy Spirit. Many other men or women have submitted to kingdom authority for the gifts of heal-ing. Walking in divine health is another example of divine healing. Everywhere Yeshua went, He healed them *all*.

Smith Wigglesworth walked in the gift of working of miracles. These gifts worked together. Smith was like Peter. Everywhere he walked, there were miracles. A miracle is usually defined as something not usually attainable with natural means. Yeshua performed a miracle when He healed and touched the lepers and the woman with the issue of blood.

Prophecy is a gift. Some prophets are to a congregation, others to a nation, a city, or a spiritual purpose. Prophecy will *never* oppose the Word of God. I have heard prophecy that was not from the Holy Spirit. A prophecy should be a confirmation, not a first-information message. Any prophecy *must* line up with the Word, not make it fit to satisfy a personal desire.

Discerning of Spirits provides understanding of spirits from both kingdoms, discerning the evil spirit of a demon as Yeshua did frequently. Another example would be seeing angels, the ability to see a sickness attached to a body in the form of a spirit or an addictive spirit attached to an individual. The phrase "monkey on your back" would certainly be an example.

Speaking languages you do not know, diverse kinds of tongues reminds me of Smith Wigglesworth who walked up to several men at the train station, began to converse with them in their own language, and led them the whole group to the Lord. He did not realize until later when it was related to him by a witness. He spoke their language which he did not know. Speaking in tongues can be a totally heavenly language or an earthly tongue, which another may understand. An interpreter of tongues may be either language. The heavenly language is for your own edification, not intrusive or out or order in a service.

The Holy Spirit gave gifts of ministering to the body of Christ to edify, build up, and guide the ecclesia. Understanding the gifts Holy Spirit bestows upon individuals demonstrates diversity of growth in the body of Christ. Everyone does not have the same manifestation of the gifts. Each gift is from Holy Spirit and may manifest differently in each personality. None of the gifts of Holy Spirit have vanished. They are not to be feared but expected for spiritual body growth. Attending a church where none of the gifts are active produces a dry hole in the spirit of a man.

> If any man speak, let him speak as the oracles of
> God; if any man minister, let him do it as of the
> ability which God giveth: that God in all things
> may be glorified through Jesus Christ, to whom
> be praise and dominion for ever and ever. Amen.
> (1 Peter 4:11 KJV)

Speaking through the Spirit is like sticking your finger in a light socket. You get results. The Spirit knows what is in the hearts of men and women in the congregation or group. He also knows what will awaken a heart to salvation, deliverance, or the infilling of Holy Spirit.

Gifts given us by Holy Spirit are not a matter of personal pride; you had nothing to do to deserve the presence of God in your spirit. You choose to love and serve God and become a sacrifice willing to trade your life for His. He chooses whom He can trust to use the gifts wisely.

> I beseech you therefore, brethren, by the mercies
> of God, that ye present your bodies a living sac-
> rifice, holy, acceptable unto God, which is your

reasonable service. And be not conformed to this world: but be ye transformed by the renewing of your mind, that ye may prove what is that good, and acceptable, and perfect, will of God. For I say, through the grace given unto me, to every man that is among you, not to think of himself more highly than he ought to think; but to think soberly, according as God hath dealt to every man the measure of faith. For as we have many members in one body, and all members have not the same office: So we, being many, are one body in Christ, and every one members one of another. Having then gifts differing according to the grace that is given to us, whether *prophecy*, let us prophesy according to the proportion of faith; Or *ministry*, let us wait on our ministering: or he that *teaches*, on teaching; Or he that *exhorts*, on exhortation: he that *gives*, let him do it with simplicity; he that *rules*, with diligence; he that *shews mercy*, with cheerfulness. Let love be without dissimulation. Abhor that which is evil; cleave to that which is good. Be kindly affection one to another with brotherly love; in honor preferring one another.

Let no man despise thy youth; but be thou an example of the believers, in word, in conversation, in charity, in spirit, in faith, in purity. Till I come, give attendance to reading, to exhortation, to doctrine. Neglect not the gift that is in thee, which was given thee by prophecy, with the laying on of the hands of the presbytery. Meditate upon these things; give thyself wholly to them; that thy profiting may appear to all. Take heed unto thyself, and unto the doctrine; continue in them: for in doing this thou shalt both save thy-

self, and them that hear thee. (1 Timothy 4:12–
16 KJV)

Even the youth will be filled with the presence of the Lord. Joel 2:27–29 (KJV) tells us there will be a day even the youth will prophesy. We shall have dreams and have vision filled with His Spirit.

> And ye shall know that I am in the midst of Israel, and that I am Yahovah your Elohim, and none else: and my people shall never be ashamed. And it shall come to pass afterward, that I will pour out my spirit upon all flesh; and your sons and your daughters shall prophesy, your old men shall dream dreams, your young men shall see visions: And also upon the servants and upon the handmaids in those days will I pour out my spirit. (1 Timothy 4:12–16 KJV)

The gifts are alive and well today. Timothy was told to neglect not the gift given to him and to meditate day and night upon the Lord. The closer we are in our relationship, the easier to be used through Holy Spirit's spiritual gifts. We need to pursue the Gift Giver, not the gift, and they will be manifest in our lives.

Fruit of the Spirit

The fruit of the Spirit is *love*. All else is a description of love demonstrated in our lives. When Yahovah described Himself in Exodus expressing every trait listed in the New Covenant; Exodus was quoted by Paul in Galatians, Ephesians, and Colossians and referred to by James.

> And Yahovah passed before him and proclaimed, "Yahovah, Yahovah Elohim, merciful and gracious, longsuffering, and abounding in goodness and truth, keeping mercy for thousands, forgiving iniquity and transgression and sin, by no means clearing the guilty, visiting the iniquity of the fathers upon the children and the children's children to the third and the fourth generation." (Exodus 34:6–7 NKJV)

Fruits of the Spirit are quoted in Galatians 5:22–23 (NKJV),

> But the fruit of the Spirit is love, joy, peace, longsuffering, kindness, goodness, faithfulness, gentleness, self-control. Against such there is no law.

> For you were once darkness, but now you are light in the Lord. Walk as children of light (for the fruit of the Spirit is in all goodness, righteousness, and truth), finding out what is acceptable to Yahovah. And have no fellowship with the

unfruitful works of darkness, but rather expose them. (Ephesian 5:8 NKJV)

Therefore, as the elect of Elohim, holy and beloved, put on tender mercies, kindness, humility, meekness, longsuffering; bearing with one another, and forgiving one another, if anyone has a complaint against another; even as Christ forgave you, so you also must do. (Colossians 3:12 NKJV)

But the wisdom that is from above is first pure, then peaceable, gentle, willing to yield, full of mercy and good fruits, without partiality and without hypocrisy. Now the fruit of righteousness is sown in peace by those who make peace. (James 3:17–18 NKJV)

Fruit is the result of good seed planted in the heart and allowed to be watered, fed, and nurtured by *love*. From the beginning, Yahovah's love is expressed in our relationship with the Creator.

I love it when wisdom as in Proverbs 8:22–30 was there from the beginning. I believe love was *first*. Love is found 541 times in the Bible. Elohim allowing Adam and Eve to live after betrayal was love in action to keep them from eating of the second tree.

Yahovah possessed me at the beginning of His way, Before His works of old. I have been established from everlasting, from the beginning, before there was ever an earth. When there were no depths I was brought forth, when there were no fountains abounding with water. Before the mountains were settled, before the hills, I was brought forth; While as yet He had not made the earth or the fields, or the primal dust of the world. When He prepared the heavens, I was there. When He drew a circle on the face of the deep, When He established the clouds above, When He strengthened the fountains of the deep, When He assigned to the sea its limit, So that the waters would not transgress His command, When He marked out the foundations of the earth, Then I was beside Him as a master craftsman; And I was daily His delight, Rejoicing always before Him, Rejoicing in His inhabited world, And my delight was with the sons of men. "Now therefore, listen to me, my children, for blessed are those who keep my ways. Hear instruction and be wise, and do not disdain it. Blessed is the man who listens to me, watching daily at my gates, waiting at the posts of my doors. For whomever finds me finds life, and obtains favor from Yahovah; But he who sins against me wrongs his own soul; All those who hate me love death." (Proverbs 8:22–36 NKJV)

Paul tells us without love, we are a resounding gong or a clanging cymbal. "If I speak in the tongues of men and of angels, but have not love, I am only a resounding gong or a clanging cymbal. If I have the gift of prophecy and can fathom all mysteries and all knowledge, and if I have a faith that can move mountains, but have not love, I am nothing" (1 Corinthians 13:1 KJV).

As a believer, we need to express His love through us. Wisdom is always there. If we lack wisdom, we only need to ask as in James 1:5; if we lack love, we are not in relationship with our Redeemer. "*And if any longs to be wise, ask God or wisdom and He will give it. He won't see your lack of wisdom as an opportunity to scold you over your failures but will overwhelm your failures with His generous grace*" (James 1:5, TPT).

God is love. "*He that loves not knows not Elohim; for Elohim is love*" (1 John 4:8 NKJV).

REDEMPTION

The Lord had saved my life several times before I moved to Oregon. Once a man confronted me with a rifle in his arms as he angrily explained he did not want me in his territory any more. The area was not his either. No problem; I left. Another time, a stranger decided my neck needed his attention. I heard a voice tell me to play dead. I suddenly went limp. When he thought I quit breathing, he dropped me on the ground and walked away thinking I was dead.

Months later, someone loosened the lug nuts all four tires on my vehicle. When I drove away, I felt the vehicle was out of sync somehow. A very twisting road was ahead. I pulled over, jumped out, and discovered two tires were almost off the hubs. I struggled to tighten all the lug nets on the side of the road and slowly left the area. My tight would not be air gun tight. Two accidental overdoses on prescription medication brought things in to focus. I had to change. Getting right with Yahovah was a lifesaving decision.

I credit Kenneth Copeland for saving my spiritual life. Saturday morning was usually a bustle of activity in the apartment complex where I lived. This Saturday was absolutely silent. I stepped outside. There were no car, truck, or train noises. I heard no children playing or bouncing the basketball against the building, no birds, planes, or barking dogs. I rushed back inside and grabbed the remote, flipped on the TV, and Kenneth Copeland was preaching. My immediate thought was, *Wow, at least someone else didn't leave in the rapture.* I listened, prayed, and became a new creation.

Redemption requires a kinsman redeemer, someone to buy us back from the bondage of sin, or in Ruth's case, a life of poverty. Boaz became a kinsman redeemer for Ruth after her husband passed away.

> Tarry this night, and it shall be in the morning,
> that if he will perform unto thee the part of a kins-
> man, well; let him do the kinsman's part: but if he
> will not do the part of a kinsman to thee, then will
> I do the part of a kinsman to thee, as Yahovah lives:
> lie down until the morning. (Ruth 3:13 KJV)

Ruth and Boaz's story was an illustration of Yeshua buying us back via the cross, paying the full price for our redemption, paying sin's demanding price to give us life and a future.

Shortly after I moved to Oregon, my brother John called and said his best friend was in the hospital; I should go pray for him. Before I could get my things together, John called again to say he was at the hospital. The patient had flatlined, and if I was coming, do it *now*. I jumped into my pickup and raced to the hospital. When I walked into the room, his family and my brother were standing around the bed. They were waiting for his daughter to arrive before they pulled the plug on his mechanical breathing. His pastor arrived, walked straight up to the bed, and began to pray comfort for the family welcoming death. Suddenly, the spirit of God hit me. I reached across the bed, grabbed the pastor's hand in midprayer, and demanded life to return to the body. I didn't pray very long when suddenly the patient breathed a deep chest rising breath, sneezed three times, and opened his eyes, wondering why everyone was standing around his bed.

Life is a gift. We have to choose how we use the essence of life. We can either choose to accept redemption or throw it away on our own desires.

Joshua in 24:15 (NKJV) declared he chose life. "And if it seem evil unto you to serve Yahovah, choose you this day whom ye will serve; whether the gods which your fathers served that were on the other side of the flood, or the gods of the Amorites, in whose land ye dwell: but as for me and my house, we will serve Yahovah."

Yeshua is our kinsman Redeemer, our older brother, and Savior. He paid the price for us. He was sold for thirty pieces of silver, the price of a bride. He bought His bride with His own blood.

Prophetic Dreams

I know many dreams mean absolutely nothing. But there are a surplus of dreams that hold great significant importance as if Yeshua Himself is sitting in your brain—oh, wait He is! The mind of Christ is *in* us.

> Let this mind be in you, which was also in Christ Yeshua: Who, being in the form of Yahovah, thought it not robbery to be equal with Elohim: But made Himself of no reputation, and took upon Him the form of a servant, and was made in the likeness of men: And being found in fashion as a man, he humbled Himself, and became obedient unto death, even the death of the cross. Wherefore Elohim also hath highly exalted Him, and given Him a name which is above every name: That at the name of Yeshua every knee should bow, of things in heaven, and things in earth, and things under the earth; And that every tongue should confess that Yeshua the Messiah is Lord, to the glory of Yahovah the Father. (Philippians 2:5–11 KJV)

When we confess He is Lord and Savior of our lives, our body, soul, and spirit belong to Him. God gives different kinds of dreams: prophetic, warning, future, and current activities. Many prophets of the nations dream of the nations and how they affect the kingdom of God. Prophets are not limited to earthly dreams. Many have visited heaven, and some have even seen hell. Whatever the dream, it is important to ask for an interpretation from Holy Spirit. I have related several dreams above and asked for an understanding how the specific circumstances are relevant to me.

When my mom was failing in health, I had four dreams she was going away. Each was a progression of the other. My brothers and I knew it would be shortly before she joined my dad and her mom in heaven. August 22, 2020, I dreamed my brother Bob and I were out in the yard working to move some rocks. I had to go to the bathroom. As I was pulling up my pants, Mom came walking through the bedroom. I ask what she wanted, and she said she wanted to discuss the songs for her funeral. "What songs do you want?"

And she responded, "Well, Dad's favorite."

"Okay, what else?"

"I don't know. That's what we need to discuss."

When I woke up, I called Bob, and we went over to my brother John's where Mom was living. She was very lucid, and we openly discussed her funeral deciding upon some old hymns: "The Old Rugged Cross," "What a Friend We Have in Jesus," "I'll Fly Away." And I downloaded from the internet "I Want to Stroll Over Heaven with You."

Early in September, I went to bed early. I dreamed there was one of the largest men I have ever seen sitting in a chair beside my bed. My guardian angel, I am sure—good thing he is big, I need a big angel to keep me out of trouble. I was adjusting to someone being in the bedroom when I looked as mom walked through and began shuffling blouses in my closet. I asked what she was looking for. She said she needed a white blouse. I told her I didn't like her wearing my clothes. She picked up a long-sleeved white blouse, threw it over her arm, and started to walk out. I asked what she needed it for.

She responded, "As soon as I change my clothes, I'm leaving in a few minutes."

I ask where she was going. "Away."

"Who are you going with?"

She said, "I'm not sure." She walked out the door.

A month later, I dreamed Bob and I were driving up a gravel mountain road when we saw mom along the road picking flowers. She had half an armful of beautiful flowers. We both said at the same time, "Isn't that Mom?" Bob jerked the car into park; we jumped out and ran over to her. She was younger, hair fixed, and walking alongside the road with no limp or dragging her feet.

"Why didn't you tell us you were coming here?"

She said, "I told Lorraine I was coming here."

I asked where her car was. She stated, "Around the corner, it has a flat tire." We could not see it when we searched the area. We walked up around the corner, and her car was in a large tent, sure enough with a flat tire.

She said, "You need to take this girl back with you. She needs to return to the near town of Irrigon. She's not supposed to be here."

I said, "I didn't know the girl, her parents, or her phone number to take her to her parents." She was writing her phone number on my hand when I woke up.

November 4, 2020, I dreamed Mom was lying on a bed when an angel suddenly stood by her bed. He reached out to touch her arm when bright shinny oil dripped off the end of his fingers in a pile. He said, "It's time to go," and left. It was four or five in the morning. Mom passed away early that morning.

November 6, 2020, I had a vision, saw Mom and Dad walking down a very shiny street holding hands, very happy—she was with Daddy again. The Lord spoke to me, "Wear *no* black" at her funeral.

Not all my dreams are family. I had a warning dream of a male coworker who did not seem to like me. I dreamed I was swimming in a lake when I walked near the rope setting apart the open area from the deep water. Suddenly a very large shark leaped up with his mouth gapping wide open up against the rope and slid back into the water. Got my attention! I asked what that meant. The Lord revealed the interpretation. It was the coworker who wanted to remove me from the job because of jealousy; I was a woman and was making progress in my assigned position. A month later, he suddenly dismissed me without reason while my supervisor was away on job-related training.

I had another warning dream just recently of a man I knew who came to my house at 3:45 a.m. I couldn't sleep and was wandering around the living room praying when I heard a car door outside. I stepped to the side of the window to look out without moving the curtain. I saw the man step up, ring the door bell, and wait for an answer. The dogs didn't bark as he waited. He glanced toward the window, then stepped down the steps, walked up to the fence, and proceeded to urinate on the metal post before returning to his car, once more glancing at the house, and drove away. It was a warning I heeded. He is not the man he has portrayed to be.

Talking to the King in the middle of the night is thrilling and exciting to be able to hear approval and direction. I learn by experience. Recently I dreamed I was walking across a wide green field at the edge of hillside. I saw an older woman walking, followed by a much older woman stumbling and slowly walking with a cane. I could tell the first woman was ignoring the second woman. I walked up to ask where Grandma was going. She was almost tearful, stating she was ninety-nine years old, wanted to go home, and her daughter didn't want anything to do with her. I suggested we sit on a large rock, talk, and rest a several minutes. We sat on the rock next to a small river babbling over the riverbed. We talked for a few minutes when I saw a movement in the water. Suddenly three men in wet suits surfaced from the water. I told them Grandma wanted to go home. They said they would be willing to take her home. Somehow they found an old farm truck with a small stock rack. Grandma lay down in the back while they drove out of the confinement area to take her home. I followed in my car. When we arrived, I asked if anyone knew of any relatives with her same last name; they pointed to a home at the end of the road. My mom appeared there. She said she came to meet me and gave me a couple gifts before I woke up.

I didn't take long to realize I had just escorted a holocaust survivor to the promise land. Out of the river of life grounded upon the solid rock, the Father, Son, and Holy Spirit all came to accompany her home from the life of confinement and frustration. I was so excited for days I couldn't keep the dream to myself.

Traveling in dreams is common. I know my dreams have taken me to several countries, teaching, preaching, and praying for the sick. I have had dreams since I was a teenager. I did not try to understand them for years but wrote many down, hoping someday to find they had been fulfilled. Today I keep a log of all my dreams, visions, words, and even voice messages. Dreams are not be feared or forgotten. They are important. Didn't Joseph tell Pharaoh his dreams are interpreted by the Lord?

I dreamed of a trip to a large conference. It seemed to be Washington DC where a lot of believers were gathered for a strategy meeting. As we were dismissed, I needed the restroom. I asked where the facilities were. A lady pointed to a very long line. Isn't there another on this floor or on the next? She explained this was the only restroom on this floor, but she had heard there was another upstairs. I took an elevator to an empty hallway. I walked the hallway a couple of times looking for the door with some kind of marking, none. Another woman exited the elevator. As I watched her walk to the wall and opened a door, I saw wall mirrors. I finally found what I needed. As I was finishing, I saw under the wall, which was about a foot off the floor, the next stall. There was a lady wiping her very large feet with toilet paper; first one foot, then the other. I was impressed! I have never seen that before. I left, returned to the elevator, discovered I was left alone. My ride had already left. I woke up.

I understood the strategy meeting. Everyone was asking questions, taking notes, and excited about what was next. But the woman in the restroom was a quandary. Why after attending such an important meeting was she wiping her feet with toilet paper of all things? The interpretation was a bit startling. The feet represent our walk with the Lord. She was wiping her feet in self-righteous indignation. She was too big or well known to listen to such strategy, back to the religious "do it myself, do it my way" theory.

March 2022, before the tornadoes hit Texas and tore up half the state, I had a dream early in the morning. I was in a lake in pretty deep water when I looked up and saw a water moccasin, one of the south's most dangerous snakes, swimming toward me. I started to move backward when I saw a second water moccasin coming from the opposite direction. All of a sudden, both bypassed my spot, attacking each other fighting in the air above the water. Okay, I'm awake now.

I pondered the meaning all day until early afternoon when my daughter Ruth called to tell me everyone was safe and okay. I had no idea what she was referring to. She proceeded to tell me one of the most powerful EF2 tornadoes had struck Texas. When she showed me the map, it was like a long narrow slit in the wind that simply bypassed her property. Her neighbors had trees down. The only home damaged was an unoccupied home down the road. She was awakened by the sound of chainsaws clearing the road allowing people to go to work.

When asking the Lord for a sermon one day, I dreamed of an open Bible lying on a table. The pages started to slowly turn and stopped at Colossians 3. I heard the Lord tell me that was to be my next sermon. He has given me other scriptures in my dreams indicating what to speak on.

Once I dreamed of myself writing checks. Each was a progression of the other. The first check was $119.57, $119.59, $119. 64. My next assignment for Sunday's sermon. The heading in KJV was "My heart is devoted to You." Psalm 119 is an acrostic Psalm. This section is Hebrew letter chet which is defined as stubborn like a donkey. Apparently there was a need in the congregation.

Dreaming is a gift. Many dreams are instructions or training grounds for our spiritual growth. Many prophets have significant dreams that affect our nation; we need to pay attention to them. A prophet need not back down from a dream from the Lord as it could change a nation or a government.

THE WEAK CHRISTIAN CONDITION

The problem with many believers is they have the self-centered, "poor me, and how can I get everything" attitude without working for it. We need patience to wait upon God to act. Everyone reminds us to not pray for patience because praying for patience could bring on trials or tribulations. We are afraid of trials because we don't really trust God to carry us through.

God wants us all to draw closer to Him, to become one with Yeshua. Our spirit wants to be closer, but our bodies are lazy and weak. We get alone to pray when the Holy Spirit reminds us of things in our lives that need change, things that hinder our relationship with the Father. We may be ready to give up sins that the world would consider a sin, such as drinking, smoking, chasing after the opposite sex; but that is as far as it goes. The more we pray, the more we desire to be closer to the Lord. The problem is we consider the little things—bitterness, gossip, not forgiving a wrong, and how they may affect healing and restoration. The real impasse begins; we quit praying by giving into the barrier that separates you from the relationship once enjoyed. Many spend their whole life praying to get closer to God or to be used by God in a greater way by giving up the brokenness; you keep putting off the answer. God keeps asking; round and round you go like merry-go-round, sometimes never getting anywhere until we ether die or just plain quit; some may even resign church because "God never answers my prayers so, why pray?" If we don't yield or submit to everlasting love, our lives will not change. The struggle would be simpler when we takes a few moments, dig for the revelation of the root of the barrier. Yield to the Holy Spirit and give it back to where it came from and walk in freedom. *Work*, but worth every moment of prayer and submission to the Love that waits.

Many wonder why God seldom seems to answer prayers. It's because we hang on to sins in life like they were best friends. By refusing to listen to the Holy Spirit's urging to surrender to God's will for our lives, we refuse to draw closer to His tender love. We stubbornly refuse His plan for us. How do we expect to see His power in our prayers, His glory being revealed through our actions? A sin is anything that hinders our close communion with Yeshua and the Father.

Paul states in Colossians 1:9–14 (KJV),

> We have been delivered from the power of darkness. That ye might walk worthy of Yahovah unto all pleasing, being fruitful in every good work, and increasing in the knowledge of Elohim; Strengthened with all might, according to his glorious power, unto all patience and longsuffering with joyfulness; Giving thanks unto the Father, which hath made us meet to be partakers of the inheritance of the saints in light: Who hath delivered us from the power of darkness, and hath translated us into the kingdom of His dear Son: In whom we have redemption through His blood, even the forgiveness of sins.

Forgiven and delivered does not mean walked on; we can walk away from a battle within ourselves by stopping the struggle, walk away to pray, then proceed with the action. Many Christians are in a continual struggle with the Holy Spirit. We are unwilling to listen and be obedient to Holy Spirit living right inside us, thereby avoiding experiencing the great power designed for any believer. Don't be afraid to pray.

The First Letter of Peter 1:7 (KJV) says, "*That the trials of your faith are more precious than Gold*." It is the trials in our life that draw us closer to God. They cause us to pray. God so wants us to talk to Him. He longs to hear our voice. As any parent longs to hear their child call their name, God longs to hear us call Abba Father. Many people really don't want to change because they receive too much sympathy, affirmation, and attention by staying broken. Others recoil because of the pain that results from revisiting the wounds that have contributed to their dysfunctional behavior.

Jude 24 makes provision for our healing our brokenness.

> Now unto Him that is able to keep you from falling, and to present you faultless before the presence of His glory with exceeding joy, To the only wise God our Savior, be glory and majesty, dominion and power, both now and ever. Amen. (Jude 24 KJV)

John 4:14 (NKJV) says, *"We are a well spring of living water. But whoever drinks of the water that I shall give him will never thirst. But the water that I shall give him will become in him a fountain of water springing up into everlasting life."*

> He who believes in Me, as the Scripture has said, out of his heart will flow rivers of living water. (John 7:38 NKJV)

> The steps of a good man are ordered by Yahovah: and he delights in his way. Though he fall, he shall not be utterly cast down: for Yahovah upholds him with his hand. I have been young, and now am old; yet have I not seen the righteous forsaken, nor his seed begging bread. (Psalm 37:23–25 NKJV)

> Cast thy burden upon Yahovah, and He shall sustain thee: He shall never suffer the righteous to be moved. (Psalm 55:22 NKJV)

Keep your heart with all diligence, For out of it
spring the issues of life. (Proverbs 4:23 NKJV)

According as His divine power hath given unto
us all things that pertain unto life and godliness,
through the knowledge of Him that hath called
us to glory and virtue. (2 Peter 1:3 NKJV)

The covenant is about promises believers can use to remove the
brokenness people live with every day. Sadly most people live with
brokenness all their lives and never know they can be restored or
repaired. The first thing is to identify some of the common brokenness people suffer with. The Bible has a lot to say about healing,
deliverance, and restoration and how we can restore the brokenness
in our lives.

I had a dream with my three brothers in July 2021. We were in
a house being somehow contained. It was not a prison, but it felt as if
we could not leave. The boys were in another room. I was in a room
by myself looking out a locked window when a man came in holding
a multitool. It was in the shape of an X with each end having a red
oval circle handle in the center. He said he was giving me a tool to
get myself out. I looked at it and asked, "What could I do with that?"

He began to explain, "If you use it one way, it was a saw. If you
use it another way it could be used as scissors. If you use it another, it
could be a shovel. Whatever you need it for, it is the answer."

Another man walked in and said, "Listen to him. It is your only
way out."

They both disappeared. I turned and saw a baby sitting on the
bed. I asked if they wanted to go on an adventure. Nodding, I picked
up the baby and jerked the bed away from the wall. I set the baby on
the floor and began using the tool prying up the floorboards digging
in the dark black dirt. The baby was sitting, watching, not able to do
a whole lot to help. I found a horseshoe pointing up. I stated, "This
would make a good shovel to move the black dirt away." I dug a large
hole, sweating and determined; I dug most of the night. I finally saw
a slight light through the dirt when I woke up.

I asked the Lord what all this meant. I knew the Bible was the multitool. I knew it was the answer to all my needs. The Lord was giving me a way out of the containment. I asked what the containment was; I thought it might represent generational iniquity in my life. Daddy used to say, "We are all a bunch of horse thieves and bastards. We need to leave the past alone." That's *not* necessarily the truth; Yahovah began to reveal things that had not been dealt with. Generational curses, events, and agreements needed to be dealt with. I had to research my family history in prayer and find the areas that had intentional or unintentional curses either spoken or acted upon. Until they are, many past curses will continue to manipulate the current generation.

Addictive behaviors—alcoholism, drug addiction, abusive behavior, certain illnesses, witchcraft, unholy alliances—can all be passed down for as long as the bloodline lasts. It benefits us to search our own heart, discover the depths of hurts, emotions, unmet expectations, wrong world views, experiences that have influenced who we think we are. Letting the everlasting love into those closets, hidden crevices, and walled-up rooms of the heart will allow the love to heal, restore, and rebuild broken walls of the soul.

The invisible thread is an unbreakable, continuous bond, "While we look not at the things which are seen, but at the things which are not seen: for the things which are seen are temporal; but the things which are not seen are eternal" (2 Corinthians 4:18 KJV). If we can see it, it's most likely not an everlasting godsent thing, a bond stronger than anything we can imagine, the truth of God's Word, a living relationship with Almighty Creator.

Brokenness is anything that stops or hinders us from a full, free, exciting, productive life with all God designed for us. Life experiences cause brokenness, some purposely and some accidental. God is always there, but we need to allow Holy Spirit to help us to work through the mental and emotional damage.

Why should people live in brokenness or bondage? Believers need to be able to live free from the past hurts and experiences which have shaped out lives. Brokenness can be a stronghold from the adversary to keep believers under his thumb, controlling their lives, keeping them from flying with the eagles living free from the oppression of this worldly environment. It is a choice to continue in bitterness of the past. Release is also a choice to fly as the eagles in the sky.

When bitterness is stockpiled, not released in forgiveness, it gives the accuser a piece of ground in our life. When I worked in prison, one of the inmates remarked, "When we hang onto the past, we are renting space to the one thing we need to let go." So true, Yeshua wants us to live a free life, not one influenced by the adversary. When trouble comes and trials invade everything you stand for, you start to rebuke the accuser; he only laughs at you. You can't rebuke the accuser from his own territory. Unless you ask for forgiveness and take back the ground you traded the accuser, Yeshua will not cross the sin barrier *you* hold up between you and Him.

Your body is a temple of the Holy Spirit, the Holy of Holies here on the earth. Who do you want to be the high priest of your temple? Yeshua is a gentleman and will only go where He is invited. Your temple has many rooms and departments. Yeshua will only live where He is welcome. The accuser, on the other hand, is a greedy controlling master. You give him one square inch, and he will take control of your whole temple. A simple stronghold will grow and grow until it will not only control but influence your decisions, what you listen to, where you go, even breaking down your health could be included. Many people have lived for many years with severe illnesses only to find Yeshua in a nick of time asking for forgiveness, turning loose sin, finally destroying the barrier that separates them from the Creator. Health was fully restored in time. It is a choice not to live in brokenness of bitterness, forgiveness, or any sin that comes between you and God.

I heard Kenneth Hagin tell of an event where he had prayed for a woman with a severely deformed hand. The Lord healed the hand; suddenly he received a word of knowledge. He spoke to the woman how she needed to forgive a certain individual when she shouted into his face. "I will never forgive them." He watched as the hand returned to its original deformed condition. God is serious about giving all to Him for our own benefit.

If someone knocked on your house door you did not know, would you invite them in? What if they said they had a need, or were very friendly, or said they had a gift for you, would you invite them into your house? Okay, they are in your house, and they are friendly; they have something you think you need or even want, so you to let them stay awhile. This person has his own chair, his own little corner of your house. Remember, you invited him in. This person we will call Sam. Sam turns out to be a clean freak and cleans his little corner of your house. His corner looks good. You let Sam stretch to the rest of that room, but only this room; stay out of the rest of your house. After all this is your house, and it is none of Sam's business what goes on in the rest of your house. Well, okay, Sam can clean the bathroom, maybe the kitchen, and dining area. Stay out of the family room where you entertain family, friends, and allow outside entertainment into your house. Sam, the accuser, will take every inch of your heart that he can seduce you into giving. The embarrassment of things some Christians allow in their homes, they would not want to see in church, things if the pastor experienced, would be run out of town for doing—pornography, X-rated movies, unholy innuendos, cursing, using the name of God in vain, betrayal, or aggressive behavior. Is there any difference to God for a saint or a pastor to sin? We are all God's children. So many Christians think they can live a passive life all week, be good when around other Christians, and all will be okay.

What do we allow in our eyes, ears? What music do we listen to, movies do we watch? Because we are adults, we think we can handle the seduction of the world. We believe we can control our reactions to emotions or human responses without losing control. This is right where the adversary wants to keep you, trusting in your own strength, not allowing the Holy Spirit to lead us into all truth, having faith and trusting God knows what is best for us.

What if this house was your heart, the temple of the Holy Spirit, and the visitor was Yeshua? Yeshua wants your whole house, every room, even the bottom drawer, or back of the closet where we keep the things we want no one to know about. God already knows! He is waiting for you to surrender the back closet to him. This is a prime example of brokenness of the world. Brokenness is one where we allow the influences of the world. The constant attacks of the accuser cause us to compromise a little more and more each time we are confronted by his seductive influence. Eventually we become comfortable with worldly thoughts going through our mind, allowing tainted thinking not offended by the lack of discernment in our lives. We set ourselves up for the plunge into the broken and lost life once again by listening to physical rather than the spiritual voice of the Holy Spirit for our guidance.

I once had a dream of a young man standing in front a long hall of many doors side by side where one had a choice to accept or reject, except the door at the end was concreted shut. The other doors were colorful and easy to open. When I asked Yahovah what the last door was, He told me it was the locked closet that he had not given to Yeshua. It needed to be blasted open and let the Son in and the bitterness out. After many faltering indecisive steps, the door was finally chipped open for healing and forgiveness to flood the room with light.

The more inward or self-centered we become, the greater brokenness we create for ourselves. Freedom is only found in others-centered thinking. As the Messiah endured humanity, His body to be beaten, battered, and hung on the cross, Yeshua was showing His great love for all people. The greater the giving of yourself to others, the greater freedom we receive. Yeshua gave His human body for all mankind only to receive a heavenly body not restricted to the sinful brokenness of earth as ours is; He fought for and received the ultimate freedom from death, hell, and the grave. Yeshua left His Father's side, then gave up His heavenly authority, deity, and glory. He became human only to be abused by the ones He loved the most, abused to the point of death of His body. The sacrifice to humanity gave back total freedom for himself to live at His Father's right side. His rightful place seated with the Father, so His creation, His beloved children, Yeshua's bride is allowed to live with Him eternally. Living in heaven, we are free from all brokenness of this world, free from the attacks of the adversary's seductive influences living eternally with Yeshua.

Paul said to live is Christ. "*For to me to live is Christ, and to die is gain*" (Philippians 1:21 NKJV). All of Paul's life was for edifying the body of Christ to become all that we were created to be.

I heard Louie Giglio preach, "Don't give the devil a place at your table." It was an awareness many invite and give permission intentionally or unintentionally to their home, work, or play. Don't give the enemy any reason to feel comfortable in your life. Build yourself up in your most holy faith as Jude states, and there will be no room for unwelcome guests. "*But you, dear friends, by building yourselves up in your most holy faith, by praying in the Holy Spirit*" (Jude 1:20).

LIFE AND DEATH

From the first moment of conception, God breathes into us a living soul, which will live for eternity. We live in the womb for nine months; we become comfortable in this confined space. This is a form of confinement. We have no ability to change. In the proper time, we are forced down the birth canal struggling against the change, fear of the unknown, causing a fight for our lives. When we finally leave our mother's womb through the birth canal, we thrust into freedom, into the arms of our mom or dad where we experience new life. The new life is all worth the transformation into this new world of experiences. Life in this new world has its freedoms and its heartaches and brokenness. In the proper time, we experience "hormons." This struggle is to resist the urge to violate God's laws for our own desires of gratification.

Once again, fear of the unknown causes a tussle in our lives. Most of us find this struggle difficult, but we must be victorious. In the proper time, we are faced with the decision—salvation by faith or a rebellious life against God, a self-willed life of our own making, life with an eternity of torment separated from God. As we face this challenge, we chose to overcome or succumb to rebellion. In God's suitable time. Our life on earth must come to an end. Again, we struggle against the change, being forced into a tunnel we have no control of. Once again, fear of the unknown increases the struggle at the end of our lives. Believers leave this world of captivity to be welcomed into the arms of our loving heavenly Father. We enter eternal freedom without pain or death. Eternity is further than our imagination, blessed to live with our Redeemer forever.

The nonbeliever is separated from God, an inconceivable time of torment in darkness. God did not create separation or hell for His creation. His love for Adam and mankind was so great He gave him the freedom to choose. God gave us His Word and Holy Spirit to supply us with all the information we need to make this choice. God wants to dwell with His creation forever. You can choose and retain your right to control your life of bondage or surrender your life to a life of total freedom in the presence of God.

Spiritual Brokenness

Not all things we call fences or boundaries are bad. There are good and bad boundaries. There are limitations that help keep us from going astray from where we belong. Fences are boundaries that let us know where a border is. We need freedom with limitations of safety untethered from cares of manipulation and intimidation in this world.

A fence may tell the farmer where his land stops and the neighbor's starts, but the fence does not tell the mole under the ground where to stop. The mole will keep digging on both sides of the fence. The mole does not accept the restrictions of the fence. When we refuse to accept the laws we are governed by, we are like the mole. We cross over into and under the authority of the other side of the fence.

The other side of the boundary may not be good for us. The other side will not allow the mole the freedoms as he knows it on the first side. All farmers have a different set of rules that control their kingdom. True love will allow the mole the right to live on whichever side of the fence he wants. The consequences are completely different on each side of the choice. Farmer number one may allow the mole to run and dig freely, but farmer number two uses poison and traps. Now the mole may live a long time on farmer number two's property without any trouble; but sooner or later, the trap will snap, and he will be caught, death by a bad choice.

The freedom of choice was given to us in the Garden of Eden by a true and loving God who created us for a walking and talking relationship with our Creator. God does not want robotic dolls for His family. Most habits or addictions start simple and even feel good to our body for a while. We generally don't know or even realize when this habit begins to control you. What you used to control now controls you. As the mole poking his head out of the ground to see the green grass looking greener on the other side of the fence, it moves closer until the trap snaps. (Remember the grass grows greener over the septic tank.) What makes the grass grow green will soon kill you. God wants people who chose His love and freedom within His kingdom who have chosen to stay within the limitless fence of His love.

Even the fence of His love is a form of boundaries, as a bond servant would choose to work for His master because of His love for the master. A master of freedom and love is a pleasure to serve; therefore the boundary can become a freedom within itself. When Townsend and Cloud wrote the book on boundaries, many refused to understand the bondage and brokenness of the soul can be restored. The Holy Spirit knows where the root of fear, codependency, anger, or the need to be in control. Letting these go may be a major spiritual battle, but finding peace in the spirit is comforting in the knowledge God has it all in His control. *We* don't need to fight God. We need to submit to His love and allow the healing balm of Gilead to flow through our hurts, unmet expectations, and soothe our broken hearts.

Many times the struggle of sin holds us into a spiraling pattern always toward darkness, out of control. We can choose to put a stop to the pain, to the helpless feeling or the vulnerability of memories. Shame is a stronghold of intimidating spirit redemption has paid the price of freedom for. Why hang onto the scabs of the past? What do these things give you that you choose to hang them in your closet? There is always a value or a reason, a payback for hanging on to a behavior.

Smoking has an artificial value to many. Their excuse that calms them down is a lie. What really is going through the mind is returning to a familiar behavior that takes me from the stress or fear of the moment. Drugs only masks the pain, never solves a situation. Needing to be in control all the time usually means one is out of control in so many areas. God gets no glory from your need to control. Like the lady who cleans the closet or kitchen over and over because that is the one area she feels in control, the rest of her life is going to hell in a handbasket. Abuse, domestic violence, and out-of-control anger are all issues that have a basic root: hurt people hurt people. Counseling is one alternative, but relying on the Holy Spirit to turn things around gives better results. You may need that counselor to help show you some options and how to proceed into the world of healing. A heart full of love solves a lot more than a tongue of vinegar.

While I worked in the prison, I taught parenting inside out. Building or courting a relationship with their child, they could send a video while reading to the child. There was a choice of several age appropriate books. One of the assignments was to write a letter to their baby's mother asking for permission at the end of the class to attend graduation. Some inmates were willing to write the letter while having a good relationship with their spouse. A few did not have that. The letters opened the opportunity to bring the children to the graduation in nine weeks. Some letters varied from outright yelling, condemning, or blasting their relationship. They were not accepted and sent back for a drastic rewrite. I reminded them honey gets more results than vinegar, to find it in their hearts to write for the benefit of the child, not the anger against the other parent. Seven weeks of redrafts eventually resulted in the child or children attending the graduation at the end of the nine weeks. The smiles and laughter of the renewed relationship were fantastic with tears all around. When a dad has several children, it is a very difficult incarceration for both parties. The visit was priceless. Using honey instead of vinegar restored parent-child relationships.

God has written His love letter covered with honey and love all over it. His Word may have correction actions spoken or impressed on our heart. These are not for punishment but drawing us into deeper relationship with our Creator. God is love, not just has love. His whole heart is to draw us into His heart. God draws, not commands us to love Him. I once heard Him say, "I love that you love me." It almost dropped me to my knees in the office.

Years ago, I was driving and talking with the Lord. I saw an indention in the seat of a passenger. I knew I was not alone. I have walked into a room filled with the sudden smell of flowery aroma.

He was there, not in the distance but reassuring me He was there to help handle any situation.

A friend suggested I read a devotional called *The Divine Romance* based on Song of Solomon by Brian Simmons and Gretchen Rodriguez. It has literally changed my life in 365 ways. Every day I hear the voice of my Redeemer telling me He loves me, I am important, I matter, I am His. The relationship we have should not be a drudgery or difficult. It should be fun, exciting, anticipating the next move. When I hear people say serving God is hard, it tells me they don't have a love relationship with the King of kings but a servitude attitude with rules and regulations. His protection is my fence of love keeping me from the tornadoes of life. Resting in His presence gives me the eternal assurance. Even if I don't feel Him, He is still right beside me in every situation, in the Holy of Holies of my heart waiting for my visit once again.

Angels

Angels are around us for protection. When we believe in the spiritual realm, we can experience their presence. I have asked for the holy angels to protect my property on all four corners. I have seen them standing as sentries around my home and office at work. While in the hospital, I knew my personal angel was there. I saw his shadow in the chair, felt his presence in the long nights while still so weak I couldn't even press the call button when I needed help.

I have seen angels in several church services. Once during worship, I saw eight tall angels standing in the back of the room worshipping with the congregation. Their voices were majestic. Seven were dressed in long white robes with yellow sashes across the chest. The eighth and center angel had a blue sash across his chest. Angels are messengers. They are sent by Yeshua to do our bidding when it is in accord with His Word. It seems I have had angels around me most of my life. When I have lost something, it suddenly appears in sight. Once an angel brought my puppy back to me; when I turned around, he had disappeared. Angels have spared me from accidents, giving traveling protection, as well as kept my home safe.

> But to which of the angels said he at any time,
> Sit on my right hand, until I make thine enemies
> thy footstool? Are they not all ministering spirits,
> sent forth to minister for them who shall be heirs
> of salvation? (Hebrews 1:13–14 KJV)

Psalm 148:5 says they are created to praise the Lord. It is taught in Judaism that the angels rise every day at daybreak to sing, "Holy,

Holy, Holy are you Yahovah," just as it is quoted in Isaiah and Revelation.

> Praise Yahovah! Praise Yahovah from the heavens; Praise Him in the heights! Praise Him, all His angels; Praise Him, all His hosts! Praise Him, sun and moon; Praise Him, all you stars of light! Praise Him, you heavens of heavens, And you waters above the heavens! Let them praise the name of the Lord, For He commanded and they were created. He also established them forever and ever; He made a decree which shall not pass away. Praise Yahovah from the earth, You great sea creatures and all the depths. (Psalm 148:1–7 NKJV)

> And one cried unto another, and said, Holy, holy, holy, is Yahovah of hosts: the whole earth is full of His glory. (Isaiah 6:3 NKJV)

> And the four beasts had each of them six wings about him; and they were full of eyes within: and they rest not day and night, saying, Holy, holy, holy, Yahovah Elohim Almighty, which was, and is, and is to come. (Revelation 4:8 NKJV)

> Let love of your fellow believers continue. Do not neglect to extend hospitality to strangers [especially among the family of believers—being friendly, cordial, and gracious, sharing the comforts of your home and doing your part generously], for by this some have entertained angels without knowing it. (Hebrews 13:1–2 AMP)

Recently I had a dream hearing voices outside; since it was raining, I did not think anyone should have been there. I opened the door and saw two older ladies outside seated and talking on the patio. I told them I didn't know they were there and asked who they were. The tall one explained she was a friend of my mom's named Ruth; the second lady indicated just came to bring a message. She suddenly left. I asked Ruth, since it was raining and beginning to be cold, if she would like to come in and spend the night, to which she agreed. We went to bed. The next morning, she was gone.

I called my brother John to see if he knew any of Mom's old friends named Ruth. He told me she had a best friend named Ruth who had passed away a few years ago. We searched the internet and found they were buried in the same cemetery. I knew then I had an angelic visitor.

Angels are messengers, helpers, and deliverers of heaven's assignments or provisions. Holy angels help us fight our spiritual battles. Elijah told his servant to look to the mountains. He saw the angel armies arrayed in battle formation.

> And when the servant of the man of God arose early and went out, there was an army, surrounding the city with horses and chariots. And his servant said to Him, "Alas, my master! What shall we do?" So He answered, "Do not fear, for those who are with us are more than those who are with them." And Elisha prayed, and said, "Yahovah, I pray, open his eyes that he may see." Then Yahovah opened the eyes of the young man, and he saw. And behold, the mountain was full of horses and chariots of fire all around Elisha. (2 Kings 6:15–17 NKJV)

Angels from Genesis to Revelation play an important part of past, present, and future. They worship around the throne 24/7 and still minister on the earth, manifesting in human form. They are not human. According to Matthew 6:30 (NKJV), angels neither marry nor have children. *For in the resurrection 'humans' neither marry nor are given in marriage, but are like angels of God in heaven.*

> For He shall give His angels charge over thee to
> keep thee in all thy ways. (Psalm 91:11 NKJV)

Angels are God's created beings. They are lower than Yeshua who has all authority over them.

> For to which of the angels did He ever say: "You
> are My Son, Today I have begotten You?" And
> again: "I will be to Him a Father, And He shall be
> to Me a Son?" But when He again brings the first-
> born into the world, He says: "Let all the angels
> of God worship Him." And of the angels He says:
> "Who makes His angels spirits and His ministers
> a flame of fire." (Hebrews 1:5–7 NKJV)

We all have guardian angels; we just don't usually have the ability to see them. It is becoming more common to hear of children telling of angels in the night or seeing angels in the room.

> And it shall come to pass afterward That I will
> pour out My Spirit on all flesh; Your sons and
> your daughters shall prophesy, Your old men
> shall dream dreams, Your young men shall see
> visions. And also on My menservants and on My
> maidservants I will pour out My Spirit in those
> days. (Joel 2:28–29 NKJV)

I believe we are in these days now.

Angels are a part of the kingdom. We do not worship them, but they are there throughout the scriptures as in Daniel 10:13 (NKJV), "But the prince of the kingdom of Persia withstood me twenty-one days; and behold, Michael, one of the chief princes, came to help me, for I had been left alone there with the kings of Persia."

Michael is also found in Revelation 12:7–9 (NKJV),

> And war broke out in heaven: Michael and his angels fought with the dragon; and the dragon and his angels fought, but they did not prevail, nor was a place found for them in heaven any longer. So the great dragon was cast out, that serpent of old, called the Devil and Satan, who deceives the whole world; he was cast to the earth, and his angels were cast out with him.

SIN

David knew sin yet became the groundwork of a king because he sought forgiveness to be the example of the mighty King relationship we all seek.

"Purge me with hyssop, and I shall be clean: wash me, and I shall be whiter than snow" (Psalm 51:7 KJV). After his sin with Bathsheba, losing the child, and being accosted by the prophet Nathan, David knew he had sinned against God in all his actions. I believe David had a very personal relationship with the King of kings.

> Have mercy on me, O Elohim, according to Your lovingkindness; According to the greatness of Your compassion blot out my transgressions. Wash me thoroughly from my wickedness and guilt and cleanse me from my sin. For I am conscious of my transgressions and I acknowledge them; my sin is always before me. Against You, You only, have I sinned and done that which is evil in Your sight, So that You are justified when You speak [Your sentence] and faultless in Your judgment. I was brought forth in [a state of] wickedness; in sin my mother conceived me [and from my beginning I, too, was sinful]. Behold, You desire truth in the innermost being, and in the hidden part [of my heart] You will make me know wisdom. Purify me with [a]hyssop, and I will be clean; Wash me, and I will be whiter than snow. Make me hear joy and gladness and

be satisfied; Let the bones which You have broken rejoice. Hide Your face from my sins And blot out all my iniquities. Create in me a clean heart, O Elohim, and renew a right and steadfast spirit within me. Do not cast me away from Your presence And do not take Your Holy Spirit from me. Restore to me the joy of Your salvation And sustain me with a willing spirit. Then I will teach transgressors Your ways, And sinners shall be converted and return to You. Rescue me from blood guiltiness, O Elohim, the God of my salvation; then my tongue will sing joyfully of Your righteousness and Your justice. O Yahovah open my lips, that my mouth may declare Your praise. (Psalm 51:1–15 AMP)

David also knew the value of confession and the release of sin and wrote another psalm of praise.

How happy and fulfilled are those whose rebellion has been forgiven, those whose sins are covered by blood. How blessed and relieved are those who have confessed their corruption to Elohim! For He wipes their slates clean, and removes hypocrisy from their hearts. Before I confessed my sins, I kept it all inside; my dishonesty devastated my inner life, causing my life to be filled with frustration, irrepressible anguish, and misery. The pain never let up, for your hand of conviction was heavy on my heart. My strength was sapped, my inner life dried up like a spiritual drought within my soul. Pause in his presence. Then I finally admitted to you all my sins, refusing to hide them any longer. I said, "My life-giving Elohim, I will openly acknowledge my evil actions." And you forgave me! All at once the guilt of my sin washed away and all my pain disappeared! Pause in his presence this is what I've learned through it all: All believers should confess their sins to Elohim; do it every time Elohim has uncovered you in the time of exposing. For if you do this, when sudden storms of life overwhelm, you'll be kept safe. Yahovah, you are my secret hiding place, protecting me from these troubles, surrounding me with songs of gladness! Your joyous shouts of rescue release my breakthrough. I hear Yahovah saying, "I will stay close to you, instructing and guiding you along the pathway for your life. I will advise you along the way and lead you forth with my eyes as your guide. So don't make it Difficult; don't be stubborn when I take you where you've not been before. Don't make me tug you and pull you along. Just come with me!" So my conclusion is this: Many are the sorrows and frustrations of those who don't come clean with Elohim. But when you trust in Yahovah for forgiveness, His wrap-around love will surround you. So celebrate the goodness of Elohim! He shows this kindness to everyone who is his. Go ahead—shout for joy, all you upright ones who want to please Him! (Psalm 32 PTP)

King David was no different than today's believers. His sin was against God and God alone. He needed to confess and accept forgiveness, receiving the new whiter than snow heart. He knew what it was to live a life in righteousness. He was not perfect, but his first instinct was to pray and seek Yahovah. I would imagine living with the sheep for seventeen years taught him to wait, to listen, and to act on the spirit within.

What is sin? Sin is defined as missing the mark such as in target practice missing the bull's eye. We are born with man stain upon the soul from Adam. Discovering we are not perfect but were created to be gives us hope that the love we crave is attainable. We may be out of place of His love but the option of family, relationship is always just a breath away. Feeling unloved, when love is so close, the offer is for everyone. We are loved and can find the target in our empty heart when we accept the only sacrifice that paid the price for our freedom.

What is transgression? Transgression is a deliberate action against a law or rule, the act of a repeating a bad behavior and not allowing God to cleanse the soul. When we choose to hang onto the very thing that holds one into sin's grasp, we transgress against the only cure available—God's love and redemption through Yeshua and the blood He shed on Calvary when He bore or carried our transgressions.

What is iniquity? Moral or gross imbalanced behavior, an action continued until it becomes a behavior or lifestyle. Many habits developed continually through generations, in the blood line of any family or individual clear back to pre-garden. I'm sure you have heard it stated, "You're just like your father or mother." Iniquity may be masked as an illness passed from generation to the next. Abuse, anger, alcohol, drugs, or physical features can be an indication of iniquity. Witchcraft is passed from generation. So are some social clubs such as Masons or their extended associations. Their membership proposes an unholy oath with practices not acceptable in biblical principles. These memberships need to be given up, the curses broken, and oaths renounced.

We all know living in sin will keep us from a relationship with the loving God through our Savior, Yeshua. So what is *sin*? This is a nasty little word with such a broad meaning. We know of the big ones—murder, rape, abuse, drugs, alcohol. What about the little things we overlook as just being part of life, things like hate, bitterness, or forgiveness, unbelief, and disobedience, the list goes on? Sin can be anything out of God's will for our lives, to miss the mark of the bull's eye in God's plan. Whether intentional or not, because of unbelief or a wrong choice, man can walk away from God, when we turn the radio sermon off when God is trying to instruct us how to live or react to life. Maybe a friend tenderly asks how we are doing, trying to speak into our lives directed by Holy Spirit. We say no before turning them and God away. We are held accountable for the knowledge we refuse to hear. God sent His messenger to you, but you refused to take the time to listen.

People think they need to fully understand what they believe before they can accept it. We don't understand doctor's instructions, but we believe and follow them. We will not always understand God's plan. That's where faith must be applied. God sent His Word into the world to instruct us, implanted His Holy Spirit in our hearts to lead us into truth; we only need to accept it by faith God knows what is best for our lives. So many people use this for an excuse to reject God because they don't understand the entire Bible, therefore rejecting the call on their lives. Knowledge of the Bible is not the answer, but knowing the author of the Bible is the key.

My brother had a friend with a photographic memory. He could tell you which page a scripture was and quote the verse verbatim. He was not a believer and refused to surrender his life to the Lord, his only excuse, too many rules.

Many go to church expecting to be served by the church. What's in it for me? Sometimes we have had a bad week and need some uplifting; this should not be every week. God's love is an action that should be channeled through our lives; Holy Spirit wants to esteem others through our lives. The believer should have already spent time in the Word, not "eating off the pastor's plate." The sermon should be confirmation of what Holy Spirit has been telling you. Intercession for the assembly will give you and the pastor a boost in the service to meet the needs of the ecclesia.

A church service usually means if you are a believer, it is not you get served; the worship and sermon is to encourage, aid, and prepare us to be able to serve others in the church. We can take this love out to the troubled world for the rest of the week. The Holy Spirit knits lives to God, this invisible love thread is stronger than any visible cord man can make. This thread held Yeshua on the cross lead Abraham into the wilderness, Noah to build a great big boat in the dessert, and many others to stand the test of faith even in the face of death.

I have had dreams of pastors who it seems had disobeyed what Yahovah was telling them. It's a hard thing to tell a servant of the

Almighty they missed the mark. It wasn't hard to have a dream. It was very difficult to expound the dream and allow Holy Spirit to touch their heart. I am not a judge, only a messenger. Their disobedience is an unintentional stumbling block to their flock, causing potential spiritual damage. No one is above another. We are all accountable to each other, but most of all to Yeshua. Pastors are always under attack by the enemy. We cannot let the enemy cause divisions in the church. Dreams are from the Lord even when it is difficult to speak them.

Recently I dreamed I was at my brother John's house when I was asked to cut a couple of men's hair which I detest to do. The first man had reddish brown hair with gray sprinkled in rather bushy or maybe natural curly. I was using hair clippers clear down to the scalp. Halfway through, he jumped up and said, "Maybe I don't want to continue." He walked around a bit, sat back down, and continued his haircut. The second man had dishwater blond hair sprinkled with gray. He sat down, and I cut his hair clear off without one word. I realized they were in authority. The first question I asked was who they were having an affair with. I did not know either of the men. I did not see their faces nor know their occupation. I know the hair is man's glory, and they were losing it all, certainly gives me something to pray about.

The struggle is to confront the situation. I once read a book called *Caring Enough to Confront* by David Augsburger. After throwing the book across the room a couple of times, I forced myself to read the book. I hated confrontation with a passion. I did not know how to confront any issue. There seemed a problem; I did not care enough about myself to confront another about their situation. Finally I understood looking in the mirror helps to acknowledge personal confrontation in order to counsel another on their situation.

Living in an abusive marriage always felt like walking on eggshells with no options. Where does one submit? Where does one draw the line? To walk humbly before the Lord is not a welcome mat for abuse. I went to the Domestic Violence Victim training where I finally learned what I had been living. What one is raised in is what one continues to expect. The group had to fill out a six-page questionnaire in the first hour. I had check off almost all the boxes completing five of the pages, crying all the way. As I began the sixth page, a lady next to me took the papers away with compassion. I had never defined what I had lived. It was just life. Being a believer did not change experiential beliefs. I needed a total revamp of my world, spiritual and personal views.

Knowing who you are *in* Christ changes who you *are* spiritually. There may not be physical changes, but spiritually we grow in lessons of faith. Every scripture is full of meaning. I was a believer, yes. Did know the relationship of love offered? *No*, I felt unworthy, unloved, and unaccepted. I was in church one Sunday when a young girl walked up to me in the back row. She handed me a scrap of paper folded over and walked away. I was trying to listen to the preacher when I slowly opened the note. It had a message that shocked my heart. "Jesus loves *you*." I was undone. Until then, I did not actually believe anyone loved me. That was the turning point in the relationship with the eternal King.

Teachers in school bring pop quizzes to test or check what we have learned. The panic in your heart the moment they say "pop quiz" is sometimes over whelming instant fear. What if I don't know the answer? What are they going to ask me to do? It is not designed to cause stress; the challenge is to determine what you have learned. God sends us little pop quizzes our way, not for His information but so we may know what we are capable of with God's help. God is sending you a challenge. Are you ready to submit to Father's loving heart for your life? I don't know what God has planned for your life, and God knows you don't like getting out of your comfort zone. But He knows how to prepare you for His future plans.

In one of John Bevere's studies, he tells us God may see you as a weight lifter who can only lift 120 pounds but has a 300-pound assignment coming your way. If this weight lifter does not work out and increase his ability from 120 to 300, he may get hurt when the challenge comes. We don't like working out in our spiritual bodies, so when the 300-pound challenge comes our way, we get hurt and blame God for our hurt. In each assignment we go through, God is trying to increase our faith to a 300-pound-plus faith. We can't sit around waiting for God to do all the work. The church is the body of Christ, so henceforth, we should be doing the work of Yeshua; we are the hands and feet of His body. He cannot do anything on earth unless each of us pray, declare, and act. Yeshua went to be with the Father and sent His Spirit to live in His earthly body, the ecclesia. Yeshua calls us to fulfill a need in His body. The same as any living cell in your body needs to be obedient to your brain, we need to be obedient to Holy Spirit. When God sends an assignment and we refuse to complete the challenge, He will send a similar challenge around until you complete it as God called you to.

The Holy Spirit has an assignment to light your path, show you the way, and share love and compassion from God. Our lessons begin when we are born. Holy Spirit will lead you to a personal relationship with Yeshua. The question is, are you going to surrender to the pull of the Holy Spirit, a loving friendship with Almighty Creator God of all existence? Will you ask Yeshua to come live in your heart? This is the best decision you can make by accepting Yeshua's free salvation and God's will for your life. The load that is lifted off our shoulders, untethered from the brokenness of this world, surpasses anything we can do for ourselves. Yeshua paid the price demanded for our souls, a price we could never pay. Yeshua changes our hearts and takes away desires that control us; we could never give up sin on our own. He removes the sin barrier, opens up a language from us to Himself called prayer. As we pray, this is a two-way conversation. We praise Him or ask Him for something. Then we wait for the answer. The Holy Spirit leads us and expects us to lead others, to be an example to the world around us. We serve God, not because we have to but because we choose to serve a loving God. His joy floods our souls; we serve God who restores our relationship with Him. We serve because of joy and peace we have in our relationship with our Creator.

The more messed up our lives were before we came to Yeshua, the greater the experience of this transformation. In those times you feel empty, longing for someone or something to fill your emptiness, you long for more of who Yeshua is, to have a relationship with your Creator. Knowledge is not enough. To know all there is to know is not enough. The accuser knows about Yeshua, knows every word of the Bible, yet does not have a loving relationship with Him. To know the entire Bible, and if you could understand it all, you would not have what it takes to live forever with Yeshua in heaven. It takes accepting Yeshua's relationship to have an eternity in the presence with God. You require a hunger to see His face, anxiously hear His voice, hold His hand, wander through life whispering His name. We can be in a world full of people and feel so alone, an emptiness that only time with Yeshua can fill. Oh, to experience a hunger for the presence of God to overwhelm you in a time of a void. In a time when you sing a song like "Open the eyes of my heart, I want to see you." Only God can open your heart, soften the crust of sin we have built around our hearts to open our spiritual eyes to see the realm of heaven working to draw us into that heavenly place of rest. When all seems lost, dry, or alone, He is always there; He never leaves us. Press in to His presence.

THE "JOB" CHALLENGE

Job was going wide open for God until his world tumbled down. We sometimes are going wide open for God until our body can't keep up. Are we really working in God's strength, or are we taking the reins in our own hands? Maybe God is just saying, "Trust me, I will show you a better way." Job lost everything that he held important to him: his children, his livestock, even his servants. The only possessions left were his land, house, and very his angry wife. Job never gave up his faith in God, knowing God had something better planned. The Job challenge may feel like you are alone, not able to communicate with friends, the brokenness of depression sets in and grips your very soul, so you wish you were never born. This is a time you are in the wilderness and God seems miles away. You question where you have gone wrong. Have faith, hold on to what God has told you, and wait. If you remember, Job lost everything, not because of Job but because God was teaching the accuser a lesson in faithfulness.

This is when you keep doing everything needed to stay in tune with God. Wait for God to restore you to your full potential. Keep exercising your body, stay active, get plenty of rest; and your mind will release the stress. Like being locked in a strange place, trapped in a cage, things are out of your control. Let God have control, and He will teach you to fly from your cage further than you have flown before. It is interesting to me that the larva of a butterfly before it even builds a cocoon has the same DNA as the butterfly. God is saying I don't see this larva as a worm but as the beautiful butterfly it will become, as God sees you as the majestic being He has created you to be. You were created to be loved by our Creator.

It is okay to go to a doctor or a Christian psychologist or counselor when needed. God uses these qualified people to do His will. The world will run to the doctor. The first sign of a problem some believers think if they see a doctor, it is a sign of little faith. We should pray first, but God does use doctors too. The doctor will at least give you the diagnosis as to what to pray. Shotgun prayers are not specific. Too many church people think to go to the doctor shows a lack of faith or even it is a sin not to trust God for the healing.

My brother Bob needed surgery on a lifelong problem in his neck some years ago. He was told by a pastor friend all he needed to do was go to a specific town down the road. This pastor's friend resided there. He could pray for Bob; he may be healed and not need the surgery. Bob's answer, when in doubt about what to do, "I serve a prayer answering, healing God. I don't think I need to go to some special person for healing when the same God is in my own church. I have faith in God not in some man's ability to pray for me." He had the surgery with great success. Trials in our life have two main purposes. First is to build our faith. Second is that God will get the glory for His work in our lives, not necessary in that order. If God healed him before the surgery, only he would know and give God the glory; but with surgery, who knows how many people see God working and give God the glory.

Yeshua healed me in the hospital—a miracle proclaimed through the county. Five medications each separately would have proven fatal; but the healing hand of God, through the prayers of people around the world, turned death into life. Only faith in the healing hand of Yeshua can we walk in newness of life. Seeing people healed and walking is amazing. As I was sitting in my office one morning, I felt impressed to take communion. I had a cheese cracker in my lunch and some grape juice. I blessed the bread and juice and immediately felt the healing course through my body. Whatever the pain trying to attack my body was gone. Yeshua can and does keep our bodies in health.

FAITH

Behold, his soul which is lifted up is not upright in him: but *the just shall live by his faith*. (Habakkuk 2:4 KJV)

For therein is the righteousness of God revealed from faith to faith: as it is written, *The just shall live by faith*. (Romans 1:17 KJV)

But that no man is justified by the law in the sight of God, it is evident: for, *The just shall live by faith*. (Galatians 3:11 KJV)

Now *the just shall live by faith*: but if any man draw back, my soul shall have no pleasure in him. (Hebrews 10:38 KJV)

But without faith it is impossible to please Him: for he that cometh to God must believe that he is, and that He is a rewarder of them that diligently seek Him. (Hebrews 11:6 KJV)

It is important to understand the righteous shall live by faith and faith alone. We cannot earn it or make it. We live it.

Many years ago, I had a dream of riding on a huge red horse. It was a magnificent animal. As we raced across a field, I could feel his muscles between my legs as his powerful legs swiftly carried us farther into the field. Suddenly he leaped into a large river and began to swim with equally powerful stokes as he carried me along in the river. I was amazed at the strong and powerful muscles as I watched them ripple beneath me. He knew where he was going and the strength it took to get there. Just as suddenly he jumped out of the river, I woke up. I knew beyond a shadow of a doubt the dream was real. I felt the wind in my hair, the water on my legs, and the sweat of the horse. I saw the strong muscles as they rippled down his side. Then it was explained. It was my faith. I had to use it. I was in the river of life, and only my faith would carry me through life's many skirmishes, lean on my faith. Faith will carry us through *everything*.

Faith grows. It's like direct deposit account at your favorite bank. You can withdraw any time you need; you know there is always enough to cover your need. The more you withdraw, the more it grows. This account, no matter how much you draw, will *never* fall into insufficient funds with a penalty.

> For I say, through the grace given unto me, to every man that is among you, not to think of himself more highly than he ought to think; but to think soberly, according as God hath dealt to every man the measure of faith. (Romans 12:3 KJV)

Lacking with drawl may cause faith to lose interest but not dissipate. Mustard seed faith starts small but grows into a huge tree with massive limbs and strength. We water it with the Word and let the Son shine on it, for faith to produce faith. Yeshua replied, "Because you have so little faith. Truly I tell you, if you have faith as small as a mustard seed, you can say to this mountain, 'Move from here to there,' and it will move. Nothing will be impossible for you" (Matthew 17:20–21 KJV).

Are you being challenged in your faith? We only want to be tested if we know all the answers. Life is not a test we study for. It is a surprise assessment to verify what you have already learned, what you would do in a surprise attack of the adversary. When God calls is your answer, "Hineni, here I am, send me." We trust Yeshua will only lead us into what He can take us through. There is the old adage "God will not give you a mission without providing the provision."

Abraham left his father and mother and family and went into the wilderness, following to a place God would show him *after* he got there, a place not built by human hand. What does that look like? What was Abraham looking for? Even Abraham did not know. He only followed wherever God directed; not that he didn't make mistakes along the way, but his heart was to listen and obey even during the hard challenges of the plan.

Do you trust Yeshua enough to allow Him to lead you into the unknown, to hold His hand, to do whatever God asks? Are we willing to go to the wilderness of life or go through the fiery cleansing furnace of this world? The fire of God's Holy Spirit cleans, purifies, and melts our fears away; the imperfections disappear, making a pure vessel usable for God's service. No one goes through life unscathed by many trials, temptations, and struggles with choices as David in Psalm 51.

Do we diligently seek God? Are we listening, being obedient? Do we revere Him, respect the God of all creation? Most of us are trapped in this brokenness of life, a career, work, too many toys for our time off, putting people and things between God and ourselves. Those who deny it are probably lying to themselves.

The world is full of counterfeits. We sometimes think only in money when we hear of a counterfeiter. We have counterfeit religions, churches, even pastors. So how do we know what is real and what is a counterfeit? The only way to know the real is to compare their theories to God's Word. Don't take someone's commentary or book about the Bible as truth; God's Word will expose a counterfeit. The more you read the Bible, the more things will start to fit together. The Bible will never contradict itself. Either you read it wrong or out of context. The verse must make sense where it is written, or it will be misinterpreted somewhere else. God gave us a clear path to follow. If the path makes a sharp bend, don't cut the corner. Stay on the path. Don't take the easy or short path. It may take you astray. You never know what is in the rough between the paths.

"Because strait is the gate, and narrow is the way, which leads unto life, and few there be that find it" (Matthew 7:14, KJV). Are you on the narrow path, or is your ritualistic religion holding you into a liturgical pattern? Is your relationship with your Savior the real thing, or have you settled for a cheap copy counterfeit knockoff, having no power?

> This know also that in the last days perilous times shall come. For men shall be lovers of their own selves, covetous, boasters, proud, blasphemers, disobedient to parents, unthankful, unholy, Without natural affection, trucebreakers, false accusers, incontinent, fierce, despisers of those that are good. Traitors, heady, high minded lovers of pleasures more than lovers of God; Having a form of godliness, but denying the power thereof: from such turn away. (2 Timothy 3:1 KJV)

When I first became a believer, I did not know the Scriptures at all. I was led astray because someone I thought I knew talked me into attending a small home church service. It was friendly, seemed open with ministry across the border into Mexico to give food and clothes. I did not realize I was in over my head until over a year later. I discovered their basis scripture was misused and misquoted to satisfy their particular desire. As I sat in the middle of my living room floor studying the Bible, I saw their scripture for what it was. I repented for being led into a much distorted cult.

If there is no power in your faith, check if you have the real gospel or a counterfeit. There is no greater brokenness than to base your whole spiritual life on a counterfeit or misguided religion. If Yeshua of the Bible is not your Redeemer, the Son of the living God, born of a virgin, who died on the cross of Calvary for your sins, go back to the beginning; be born again into the kingdom of God. It is not about religion, but a personal relationship with the living God.

> Eat thou not the bread of him that hath an evil
> eye, neither desire thou his dainty meats: for as
> he thinks in his heart, so is he: Eat and drink,
> says he to thee; but his heart is not with thee.
> (Proverbs 23:6 KJV)

My understanding of these verses is in verse 6: food from a corrupted or polluted person will turn sour in your stomach, physically or spiritually. Verse 7 says whom you hang around with, what is in their heart influences how you think, and you becoming as they are. We often think that our influence for the Lord will win them. But usually the pull of the world is stronger than you are, and the reverse happens.

Believers often allow their testimony to slip. They will talk the talk, but their actions speak much louder than their words. When we say we love Yeshua and call ourselves a believer, we should like the things Yeshua likes and hate the things Yeshua hates. What comes out of our mouths is really in your heart. If we dishonor people and do things that separate the body of Christ, the love of the Father is not in us.

> Above all else, guard your heart, for it is the well-
> spring of life. (Proverbs 4:23 KJV)

Out of the heart, the mouth speaks. Are your words lining up with the Word, or are they lining up with the adversary?

> For out of the heart proceed evil thoughts, mur-
> ders, adulteries, fornications, thefts, false witness,
> blasphemies. (Matthew 15:19 KJV)

> For from within, out of the heart of men, pro-
> ceed evil thoughts, adulteries, fornications, mur-
> ders. (Mark 7:21 KJV)

Planting good seed produces good things, but the adversary will destroy the seed if the mouth is not guarded daily.

> Those by the way side are they that hear; then cometh the devil, and taketh away the word out of their hearts, lest they should believe and be saved. (Luke 8:12 KJV)

> If you confess with your mouth, "Jesus is Lord," and believe in your heart that God raised Him from the dead, you will be saved. For with your heart you believe and are justified and with your mouth you confess and are saved. It is just as the Scripture says: "Anyone who believes in Him will never be put to shame." (Romans 10:9–11 KJV)

> And when he was come to the other side into the country of the Gergesenes, there met him two possessed with devils, coming out of the tombs, exceeding fierce, so that no man might pass by that way. And, behold, they cried out, saying, what have we to do with thee, Yeshua, thou Son of God? Art thou come hither to torment us before the time? And there was a good way off from them a herd of many swine feeding. So the devils besought Him, saying, If thou cast us out, suffer us to go away into the herd of swine. And He said unto them, Go. And when they were come out, they went into the herd of swine: and, behold, the whole herd of swine ran violently down a steep place into the sea, and perished in the waters. (Mathew 8:28–32 KJV)

So many people think because they pray and God answers their prayers, they are okay with their life in this world. If you will notice the scripture in Mathew 8:28–32, you will see even the demons of hell know who Yeshua is; and they even prayed to Him. Yeshua answered their prayer. Does this mean that the demons are saved, or will be in heaven? As the apostle Paul would say, "God forbid." To have knowledge of someone doesn't make you on a one-on-one standing with them. To have a personal relationship is to follow after or walk alongside with them, to walk and talk face-to-face with them. God wants you to think of Him as a brother, father, a personal friend, but with the respect. Honor for someone in authority that has done everything right in your eyes, someone you respect and honor with all your heart.

God temps no man according to James 1; but satan works overtime to destroy our faith, relationship, and testimony.

> Blessed is the man that endures temptation: for when he is tried, he shall receive the crown of life, which the Lord hath promised to them that love Him. Let no man say when he is tempted, I am tempted of God: for God cannot be tempted with evil, neither tempts he any man: But every man is tempted, when he is drawn away of his own lust, and enticed. (James 1:12–14 KJV)

Satan will tempt you, causing you to falter in your relationship with Yeshua, to destroy your faith in God anyway he can. God may challenge you by helping you be successful in your walk with Him. God gives us skills or talents in life for His glory. Some may see that these talents are so helpful they start giving the talent, or themselves, all the credit. We start to give more glory to the talent than the talent giver. God may test your talent. Maybe you love to sing. God has given you a beautiful voice, the talent to carry a tune with good rhythm. When fame comes, you take all the credit or take His talents and divert them into the world. Life may sideline your career when you choose inefficient people to work with. Pride will distract you from your true talents. God gives talents, skills, or gifts so His kingdom can be edified and glorified. God loves His creation so much that He will never take a gift He has given and will even let you use it for the world if you chose. Using God's gifts for the world estranges you from your relationship with Yeshua and puts you in great danger of judgment to come.

When we are not willing to give God the glory and praise for our blessings, we start to think our blessings are because of what we have done. Personal pride may allow the misuse of your blessing.

> In the light of the king's countenance is life; and His favor is as a cloud of the latter rain. How much better is it to get wisdom than gold! And to get understanding rather to be chosen than silver! The highway of the upright is to depart from evil: he that keeps His way preserves his soul. Pride goes before destruction and a haughty spirit before a fall. Better it is to be of a humble spirit with the lowly, than to divide the spoil with the proud. He that handles a matter wisely shall find good: and whoso trusts in Yahovah, happy is he. (Proverbs 16:15–20 KJV)

God tested Abraham with Isaac; Abraham's the most precious blessing. To be in a right standing with God, we must be willing to give back to God what we hold dearest to our heart. God has given you many blessings in His infinite mercy. Faith is obeying God in spite of the consequences and being obedient to God's challenges in life.

Many churches today have become "Marthas." *"And Jesus answered and said unto her, Martha, Martha, thou art careful and troubled about many things: But one thing is needful: and Mary hath chosen that good part, which shall not be taken away from her"* (Luke 10:41–42 KJV).

They are busy doing church they have missed the benefits of taking time to worship and praise, just set at the feet of the Savior. Find that place of solitude; relish the presence of Yeshua. He wants to be in our lives. Are you willing to give the Holy Spirit access to the inner parts of your heart, that hidden part no one knows about, your hidden past, deepest fears, or secrets you have told no one? God already knows! He is waiting for you to give Him access so He can heal and remove them for you.

Mary had found a better thing. We should be willing to worship and give God access to everything in our life. A true friend is to be respectful and courteous to the needs of your friend, to know their needs and desires to have a passion to bless them. Yeshua is much more than a friend. Yeshua is Creator, Provider, Savior, Lord, and King of kings; and we are to be more than a friend to Him. We are chosen to be adopted into His family, to have all rights as a son or daughter to the great and mighty Creator of all, how much more we owe Him our lives as stated in Ephesians 1:5 (KJV), "*Having predestinated us unto the adoption of children by Jesus Christ to Himself, according to the good pleasure of His will.*"

My prayer to God is to help us to understand and acknowledge all He has done for each of us. We go through life as if mere survival is all He promised. We do not give God the glory for even the breath that we breathe, the sun that shines to warm us every day, the job, or paycheck each month, or the house we live in. To God is all the glory. Elohim created everything to have a relationship with His creation only to see that relationship traded to the adversary in a quick decision over food. God sent His Son, Yeshua, to redeem us with His own blood. He gives us an opportunity to live with Him for eternity, to have a walking, talking life of peace, and harmony with Him. *To God be the glory.*

We cannot compare our lives with each other but walk by faith. I heard the voice of the Holy Spirit tell me we have to honor each other's calling and walk. What one needs in their walk will rarely be what another may need. We are all necessary in the family to work together to become the bride Yeshua is coming back for. Faith is what hold us to the cross and to the relationship we each enjoy with our God.

Spiritual Relationships

Christianity is not a spectator's sport to set on the sidelines and cheer when someone does something spectacular. God requires His children to participate in His kingdom activities, to be obedient at His calls, giving your best in the assignment set before you. Our horizontal relationships are in conjunction with your vertical relationships.

Let me clarify when a man pursues a woman, he must realize she does not want a short-term shallow relationship. A woman has a desire to have a long-term relationship; she never wants you to stop discovering who she is. The more you discover about her, the more intriguing she will become, the less you will understand about her, the more you need to pursue her. This is a never-ending task for a truly dedicated relationship. Any relationship is many layers deep; every time you think you have arrived at who this person is, another layer seams to peel off, and you discover how little you really know.

A God relationship is a vertical relationship. Yeshua wants you to continue to pursue Him as long as you live. The more you know about Him, the more you realize how much you don't know. How you treat your horizontal relationships as a friend, spouse, parent, and so on is how you will respond to your vertical relationship. If you cheat or dishonor your worldly relationships, you will cheat and dishonor your God relationship. Our time with Yeshua will never become dull or uninteresting when we pursue it with our whole heart. The closer we get to our Creator, the more alive the relationship becomes. The more we study His Word, the more we realize how much we don't know. As we peel off another layer, the relationship keeping us in suspense, another door opens to allow us one step closer to Yeshua, giving another glimpse into the kingdom of heaven.

Years ago, I heard the song "I Came Here to Stay" by Kenny Bishop. The chorus has been my personal theme song:

> Run if you want to, run if you will, but I came
> here to stay.
> When I fall down, I'm gonna try t'get up 'cause I
> didn't start out to play.
> It's a battlefield, brother, not a recreation room.
> It's a fight, not a game.
> So run if you want to, run if you will, but I came
> here to stay.

Yeshua is the *only* answer. *Yeshua cannot and will not save you if you don't accept Him as your Savior and Lord.*

No sin will be forgiven without a belief in Yeshua. Salvation is not "fire insurance." Salvation is through the blood and a belief in Yeshua and His redeeming work on the cross. The Son of God shed His blood to pay the price demanded for the penalty of sin. Only through Yeshua will your sins be forgiven or the debt satisfied. When your sins are removed from your soul, you can approach the Father. We pray through Yeshua, His Son, in the name of Yeshua, Jesus. Sin is a veil that separates us from a one-on-one relationship with our Redeemer.

God does not approve of sin but provided a method to remove our sins by the blood of Yeshua. We can be forgiven and be in the presence of God's holiness. *"For the wages of sin is death, but the gift of God is eternal life in Christ Jesus our Lord"* (Romans 3:2 KJV)

There are *no* works that can earn salvation. The path to the doorway to heaven goes through the cross via Yeshua's blood. The blood of Yeshua is pure enough to pay the price demanded for sin. The wages of sin is death. Every soul born on earth was born into sin and therefore falls short of the glory of God. We are doomed to death without a Redeemer dying for us worthy of the price, a sinless life for a sinful life. The price was paid for our sins. The only thing we need to do is to accept the gift given. The love of Yeshua is greater than any sin.

> And as Moses lifted up the serpent in the wilderness, even so must the Son of Man be lifted up: That whosoever believeth in Him should not perish, but have eternal life. For God so loved the world, that He gave His only begotten Son, that whosoever believeth in Him should not perish, but have everlasting life. For God sent not His Son into the world to condemn the world; but that the world through Him might be saved. (John 3:14–16 KJV)

> For when ye were the servants of sin, ye were free from righteousness. What fruit had ye then in those things whereof ye are now ashamed? For the end of those things is death. But now being made free from sin, and become servants to God, ye have your fruit unto holiness, and the end everlasting life. For the wages of sin is death; but the gift of God is eternal life through Jesus Christ our Lord. (Romans 6:20–23 KJV)

We don't need to live in the brokenness of sin of our choice. Yes, we have sins of our choice, sins that please our bodies. Our bodies love to be pleased, live a life of comfort; but what pleases the flesh most generally conflicts with our souls, displeasing God. We struggle repeatedly in our emotions, choices, and experiences, the flesh against the soul, the world against heaven, good versus bad. The one that wins is the one you feed the most.

This reminds me of the story of the old Indian that would travel from town to town with two dogs, a white dog and a black dog. He would have the dogs fight each other and have people place bets on which would win. The Indian would always win, so they asked him how he knew which would win each time. The Indian said, "It was simple, the winning dog would be the one I fed that week." What is your pleasure, to feed the whims of your body or to feed and enrich your spirit with praise, and worship, filling your soul with the Word of God?

We were designed to have a personal relationship with Yahovah; sin got in the way. Adam and Eve traded the earth and all mankind to the accuser for a bite of fruit. It seemed pleasing to the eye and filling to the body; their flesh won that fight. Mankind has been in sin ever since. But Elohim had a better plan and sent Yeshua to purchase us back, restoring a relationship with our Creator, to walk and talk as Adam and Eve enjoyed in the garden.

Is Seeing Believing?

Some people must see a miracle to believe that miracles still happen. God is still on the throne, and His Word says God never changes; He is the same yesterday, today, and forever. *"Jesus Christ the same yesterday, and today, and forever"* (Hebrews 13:8 KJV).

> So then, tongues are not a sign for believers, but a miracle for unbelievers. Prophecy, on the other hand, is not for unbelievers, but a miracle sign for believers. (1 Corinthians 14:22–25 TPT)

Miracles are for the unbeliever as stated in John 4:48 (AMP), *"Then Jesus said to him, Unless you [people] see [miraculous] signs and wonders, you [simply] will not believe."*

Religion makes it hard to believe what the Bible says. God's Word states He raised the dead, healed the sick, cleansed the leper, turned water into wine, and saved the lost. If we can believe in the creation of all existence by a loving God, we should be able to believe in His power to do miracles. If God did miracles in the past, He will do them today.

We do not need to see a miracle to believe. Yeshua told Thomas that those that believed without seeing were blessed.

> Now Thomas, called the Twin, one of the twelve, was not with them when Jesus came. The other disciples therefore said to him, "We have seen the Lord." So he said to them, "Unless I see in His hands the print of the nails, and put my finger

into the print of the nails, and put my hand into His side, I will not believe." And after eight days His disciples were again inside, and Thomas with them. Jesus came, the doors being shut, and stood in the midst, and said, "Peace to you!" Then He said to Thomas, "Reach your finger here, and look at My hands; and reach your hand here, and put it into My side. Do not be unbelieving, but believing." And Thomas answered and said to Him, "My Lord and my God!" Jesus said to him, "Thomas, because you have seen Me, you have believed. Blessed are those who have not seen and yet have believed." (John 20:24–29 NKJV)

We live in a time of doubters, people who just don't believe anything until they can see, hear, feel, and experience it for them to believe it. A good many people today need to hear of someone dying, going to heaven, returning to life, and telling the store to believe in heaven. Many believe someone's story rather than the Bible, the infallible Word of God.

What is a miracle anyway? A supernatural event, an event not explicable by natural or scientific law? What may appear supper natural to one person may not be to someone else. There must be a standard. Many use science to define what is natural or not. Science is not always right. Why not go to the Creator to ask what is natural or not; God's Word has the answer.

If we had an automobile that needed help, we would go to the dealer to get it fixed or at least go to repair manual written by the maker for our information to get it fixed. Many people, created by Elohim, avoid His owner's manual for their lives. Every excuse is used to avoid reading the truth: I can't read very well. I don't understand what I read, or it's hard to understand. Whatever the excuse may be, the Holy Spirit will give the understanding. Having book knowledge is not enough, but experiencing the truth in your heart will change how you approach the living Word of God.

A person from two hundred years ago would think most everyday events today are miracles. A car is being driven or a plane flying, walking on the moon, or a rapid fire gun shooting would all be miracles to them. We cannot see what God has in store for the future events, but I am sure many will see our future as being a miracle. Microwaves, cell phones, automatic security, even remotes with several functions were nonexistent only a few short years ago. Miracles have never vanished. The Creator is the same today as He was six thousand years ago when He opened the Red Sea in Exodus, brought manna and bird dinners for 2.5 million people.

The book of James says to count our trials in the faith as precious. Trials help us to see we need help beyond what we can accomplish on our own; we need our Creator to overhaul our problem in a way preparing us for His kingdom. Without the reality of our need for a Savior, we continue in great brokenness of self-reliance, pride, thinking we are okay. We are lost without God; trusting in our own ability for salvation only makes us work with no return of the covenant.

> Knowing this, that the trying of your faith works patience. But let patience have her perfect work, that ye may be perfect and entire, wanting nothing. If any of you lack wisdom, let him ask of Elohim, that giveth to all men liberally, and upbraids not; and it shall be given him. But let him ask in faith, nothing wavering. For he that wavers is like a wave of the sea driven with the wind and tossed. For let not that man think that he shall receive any thing of Yahovah. A double minded man is unstable in all His ways. Let the brother of low degree rejoice in that he is exalted. (James 3:3–9 KJV)

We were created by a loving, wise Creator who knew each of us before birth. He knows our trials, tribulations, and choices. His provision for us in His covenant requires faith in the Word of God no matter the situation. Love is built into our nature, but redemption brings His love alive because Yeshua paid the price on a cruel cross at Calvary.

LIFE'S BROKENNESS

The progression of our physical life from the moment of our conception is a living soul grows, learning, and maturing into a complete baby in the fullness of time. This baby develops and goes through the trial of its life. It is forced through the mother's birth canal into the freedom of open space we call earth, free from the confines of the womb, free to stretch, breathe, eat, cry, free from confining restriction, experiencing freedom, growing in the fullness of life, free from one confinement, entering into an even greater challenge facing childhood, a living soul growing, learning to walk, talk, read, write, sing, and learn of the limitations of living life in this world.

Eventually this child by the Holy Spirit will be introduced to Yeshua. Decisions, decisions, decisions—this too is the beginning of another challenge, another struggle to choose which life will this person choose for eternity. The choice to live in the light of our Creator or in the darkness continuing in the brokenness brought on by sin, corruption, and the curse of mankind because of the actions of Adam and Eve in the Garden of Eden. As a baby resists, kicks, and screams while coming into this world and into its mom and dad's arms to find the peace it was looking for, most of us do the same thing when given the choice to surrender to God, to nestle into the loving arms of God our Creator.

As the child matures and meets someone of the opposite sex, suddenly fascination stirs in the emotions. Not everyone will find that love of another person that draws our attention or catches our eye, one we choose to spend more time with them than any other person. We begin to feel we don't want to live the rest of our lives without a mate close to our heart. The couple chose to get married to become one in soul, mind, and actions. This is a form of freedom and yet constraints. It is freedom from the pursuit of searching for a mate while conforming to the will of another, soul mate. They may be someone from a different culture, raised with different standards, and ideals of family customs.

As a single person, you can go when and where you want to, read, pray, and praise God whenever as you please. You can even go to church seven days a week or do church activities full-time if it pleases you. Now you have a spouse. We just became one, and your spouse has needs influencing your time and energy. Their desires are an impact in your heart. Your time is divided. You choose to make your spouse happy, and at the same time, live my own life. The challenge can be overwhelming and overcome when both spouses give of themselves to each other, to exalt each other as being greater than yourselves. These two can dwell in the comfort of each other; the challenges of marriage can be overcome. If we put these challenges in the right perspective, the relationship will grow deeper and closer together with God. When the needs of your spouse become the center of our attention while focusing on God with all our heart, you will be freed to become the team to fulfill God-given assignments.

Before having a relationship with Yeshua, most of us kicked and screamed until we surrendered to Christ just as we did to when we came into this world. We struggled to make the right decision as to who is the right mate. We ask ourselves, do I even want to be married to someone for the rest of my life? These questions make a battle that requires an answer from God's plan. Always a challenge before we enter into the unknown.

The relationship between being born, finding our way in life, and finding the right mate while questioning do we have children or not and still submitting unto God in it will always be a struggle. As the relationship between ourselves and Yeshua grows stronger, we get closer together as we will with our future mate. One day, as the end of our time grows short, God draws us closer to Himself. God calls you in His presence, home to be with Him for eternity.

When a believer dies on earth, only their physical body dies; the spirit is united in heaven with a spiritual body similar to Yeshua's, a heavenly body, one that will not grow old nor wither away. Each step of the journey from conception to eternity is all in God's hands. Oh yes, we make choices that influence every step, but the Holy Spirit is there leading you to His will. We don't need to suffer from wrong choices.

Jesus gave Bob a beautiful song in the middle of the night. While he was sleeping, he heard Yeshua begin to sing:

> As the words echoed through the forest
> As if the song were coming from a tree.
> Now child will you live for me?
> I gave you your breath to breathe
> I gave you the cloths on your back
> And all the food that you need
> Now child will you live for me?
> I gave you victory over your enemy's
> Took away your penalty for sin
> I went to the cross so we could live together again
> Now child will you live for me?
> Will you feed my lost sheep?
> Will you Care for the little lambs
> Give water to the lonely orphans
> Now will you live for me?
> I have built for you a mansion
> I am coming back just for you
> I have given you the Spirit with love
> Now will you live for me?

Many times, I hear music in my heart. Some songs just jump out and grab the heart. I have awakened with a song ringing in my mind that just repeats over and over until I finally realize He is singing me a song. "To know, know Him is to love, love Him and I do" floated through my subconscious for days like a broken record over and over. Another song floated through the air during a therapy session. As I listened I heard "could I have this dance with you" on the overhead music system. All I could do was cry and say, "Yes, let's dance."

ANOTHER NIGHT WITH THE FROGS

Exodus talks about Yahovah sending Moses to rescue His people the Israelites from Egyptian's slavery. First, Yahovah had Moses and Aaron demonstrate His power over the Egyptians by turning Moses's staff in to a snake, then by turning the Nile River to blood. When Pharaoh refused to release Yahovah's people or even summit to Yahovah, He sent many plagues and then frogs into the land of Egypt. There were frogs everywhere even in Pharaoh's bed and ovens of the kitchen. The frogs were a pesky mess to the point of being a health hazard. Finally Pharaoh called Moses and Aaron to remove the frogs. Moses asked Pharaoh, "So you know Yahovah has power and is controlling the frogs, when do you want the frogs removed?" Even though the frogs were an intolerable nuisance to Pharaoh and his people, Pharaoh said, "Tomorrow," another night with plague of the frogs, another night with little sleep, no peace, pesky frogs hopping in and out of His bed, his servants picking them off.

Why would anyone want to have another night of misery when the problem could have been solved immediately by just submitting to Yahovah's request? The dead frogs produced a massive amount of fly larvae which developed into flies, fleas, and gnats. What a smelly mess.

The real problem so many people in brokenness need to real-ize they *are* broken. They need to recognize what this brokenness is doing to their life, the life of the people around them. Brokenness is more that they can handle by themselves. Unfortunately we are deceived into thinking I can handle this. It isn't really a problem. I can quit anytime I want.

> Ye are of your father the devil, and the lusts of your father it is your will to do. He was a murderer from the beginning, and stands not in the truth, because there is no truth in him. When he speaks a lie, he speaks of his own: for he is a liar, and the father thereof. (John 8:44 NAS)

The accuser is the father of lies and deception, the master of deceit, confusion, masquerading around claiming to be truth. Most brokenness will sooner or later destroy your life and build a wall between you and God. The accuser is the master telling us we are okay. Everything in our life is what God wants us to do or to be. Oh yes, we know there are maybe a few little things we need to work on. God knows I am human. Many tell themselves God would not refuse me to go to heaven with a little sin in my life. Would He? God set a pattern for us to follow. Even the best individual falls short of righteousness without Yeshua's sacrifice on the cross. No one qualifies to go to heaven.

Addiction is anything out of your control: drugs, alcohol, tobacco, gossip, or gambling. Anyone dealing with an addiction has an addiction of choice. The lie comes when we think if I just kick this habit, all will be okay. The problem is not the addiction. The real problem is, why did we start the addiction? What is the root of the addiction? The root could be emotional, spiritual, experiential, and even self-inflicted. Until we deal with the root of the problem, changing our addiction only changes our lifestyle, but we are still addicted to the behavior. Let me demonstrate with this story.

Bob had a relative that wanted to change their living conditions because of drug problem. The relative asked if they could stay with him for a while to help them to get a new start. This relative did move in with him. They soon had a place to move into on their own. This person's drug of choice wasn't available; they started watching X-rated movies, horror movies, mind-boggling, destructive movies all day long, anything to keep their mind as confused as the original drug of choice.

An addictive personality will continue to find an addiction until delivered from the reason for the compulsion in the beginning even if the foundation is from birth on. Drug babies, family influences, and abuse may have precipitated an addiction. In the end, the user must discover the root to be delivered from the behavior. Covenant promises include peace of mind, body, and soul.

I quit smoking forty years ago when I asked myself why I smoked. I suddenly realized my motivation came from the need to be accepted by the crowd I hung around. When it dawned on me where the addiction came from, I quit cold turkey, never picking up another cigarette. I did not like the flavor, the horse breath, or the smelly clothes. It was a relief to quit. That may be a small addiction, but I know some who like smoking to the extent they would rather die than quit. And so they do. That addiction was a whole lot easier to break than others I hung onto for many years. Praise God for deliverance.

Unless we deal with the deep-seated root of the problem, changing our drug of choice will not lift us from the gut-wrenching pull of the addiction. Addictions are a cover-up for lack commitment to the responsibilities in life. When life issues overwhelm, it is easier to turn to an emotional escape behavior, another lie of the adversary. It would be easier to submit to God's plan for your life. Many choose to live overwhelmed with addiction going down a road destined to eventual destruction. God can and does remove addictions from people's life when we submit to Him. God will not take anything away if we believe we like it. God could clean us up when we realize how destructive this is to our health, to our testimony, and how dishonoring our life is to God. When we give our whole life to honor God and all He stands for by repenting for the rebellious life, God's love openly responds.

Man was created in God's image to be an example of who God is and what He can do for mankind. The accuser hates anything that reminds him of the Eternal Father; therefore, he puts all his effort into destroying anything that looks or acts like the Father or His

Son. If the accuser can keep us focused on brokenness, we lose focus or worship on our Creator. When we emphasize brokenness created by the adversary, oppression in our lives, we are giving praise to the accuser. He exalts in his trademark—steal, kill, and destroy praise instead of magnifying the Creator.

Many times we are like Pharaoh. We want to hang on to our addictions as long as we can, such as another night with the frogs. Maybe I will turn loose, only to find oneself deeper into the adversary's snare, making it harder to turn loose. Another night with the frogs, another night with what we think is gratification when all the time blinders cover our eyes to the truth destruction brings absolute brokenness into our lives. All worldly attachments separate us further and further from the love of God.

> Now to the King eternal, immortal, invisible, to God who alone is wise, be honor and glory forever and ever. Amen. (1 Timothy 1:17 NKJV)

Our Creator, the eternal King, is the only wise and invisible given love with single-mindedness, including both parties as participants. When the love relationship is accepted, the spiritual freedom He gives is lavished in the heart. Sudden explosive, undeniable love floods the soul with peace and joy. The adversary may continue to challenge the relationship, but Yeshua promises He will overcome life's obstacles; we must cooperate with Holy Spirit. It takes a few years to get past the baby stage development as a physical child. The same principle may work in the spiritual. *But* we have an advantage with *now* faith. I don't have to wait until I am an adult to move in the spirit of God.

The covenant has many facets all based upon love of the Creator for His children and the bride. When we discover the various tools, we become stronger in our faith. The gifts were given to edify the church to become spotless and without blemish combined with the provisions of the covenant. We can live a victorious life. We, as believers, have lived below our privileges for far too long. Taking the love-filled blood covenant as part of our heritage gives us the ability to thrive in our scripted destiny. It's in His book.

I believe Yeshua is here and now. Let your faith grow in your relationship with our Redeemer, giving you the overcoming power to become the partner in the dance you were created to be. Let me put my feet on His as He twirls me around the floor, swaying this way and that, His hand on my back as I lean against His shoulder following the slightest touch of His fingers. Put on another waltz. Let's dance.

All references used are from the following:

KJV—King James Version

Kenneth Copeland Ministries, Inc.; All rights reserved. Reproduction in whole or part without written permission is prohibited. Printed in China 1991

TPT—The Passion Translation

New Testament Psalms, Proverbs and Song of Solomon Second Edition; Published by Broadstreet Publishing; Copyright 2018 Passion & Fire Ministries, Inc.

AMP—The Amplified Bible

Copyright 1987; The Zondervan Corporation and
The Lockman Foundation

NAS—New American Standard

The Lockman Foundation Copyright 1975;
La Habra Ca.

NJKV—New King James Version

Copyright 1994 Thomas Nelson, Inc.

Strong's Exhaustive Concordance

Copyright 1890 by James Strong; Madison NJ
Keyword Comparison copyright 1980
by Abingdon

***Contributed by Pastor Bob Davis, Stanfield OR**

ABOUT THE AUTHOR

Lorraine was raised on a farm in North Idaho's mountain country. She joined the USN and was stationed in Bainbridge, Maryland, until she transferred to San Diego, North Island, California. She has four daughters who live in Texas. She moved to Stanfield, Oregon, late in 2018 to a become pastor in the local churches. Lorraine has a bachelor's degree in theology from Columbia Life School of Theology, graduated from Good Samaritan Counseling Ministries, and a degree in human services management from University of Phoenix. She has become an independent Holy Spirit-filled believer in the covenant.

Author can be reached by writing to
P O Box 1619
Hermiston OR 97838